Roses from Concrete

Nadine N'Tasha Richards

Roses from Concrete

A Black Feminist Leadership Model for School Reform

PETER LANG
New York - Berlin - Bruxelles - Chennai - Lausanne - Oxford

Library of Congress Cataloging-in-Publication Control Number: 2024019996

Bibliographic information published by the Deutsche Nationalbibliothek.
The German National Library lists this publication in the German
National Bibliography; detailed bibliographic data is available
on the Internet at http://dnb.d-nb.de.

Cover design by Peter Lang Group AG

ISBN 9781636677569 (paperback)
ISBN 9781636677576 (ebook)
ISBN 9781636677583 (epub)
DOI 10.3726/b21981

Published by Peter Lang Publishing Inc., New York, USA
info@peterlang.com—www.peterlang.com

This publication has been peer reviewed.

This book is dedicated to the most precious gift from God, my son.

To my son, Sherif "Reef" Wheeler (1993-2021). Being your mother has given my life purpose and illuminated the true essence of dedicating oneself to goodness and humanity. You touched countless lives, leaving behind a profound legacy of love. Your radiant spirit, unwavering courage, and boundless love continue to inspire me, this work and so much more. May this book uplift and empower those who, like Reef, believe in a brighter, more equitable future. #LLReef

CONTENTS

PROLOGUE: FRAMING THE JOURNEY—THE RESEARCHER'S PERSPECTIVE

Research is formalized curiosity. It is poking and prying with a purpose.[1]

—Zora Neale Hurston, Dust Tracks on a Road (1942)

By the nature of my identity and profession as a Black woman and education executive leader, I have a clear connection to the research topic here. My life experiences, especially my unexpected hardships, have fueled my passion and commitment to exposing and influencing changes regarding Black women's leadership invisibility in schools.

My journey into this research began long before I embarked on this formal study. Born in Jamaica, West Indies, and moving to Brooklyn, NY, as a young child, I was regarded as an immigrant in the States and a foreigner in my birth land. In America, I quickly learned to assimilate to survive. I remember my teacher who told me I was saying my own name incorrectly. No longer Nædine (nuh-deen), I became Nādine (nay-deen). I was 7 years old then. Teachers mocked my accent, and their ignorance of intercultural humility made school officials some of my least favorite people. The same held true in high school, where I began to embrace my identity and celebrate my uniqueness as I defended my differences.

My people skills made me a convincing advocate, but I often felt like I was growing up in a home and school where it was not OK to question authority. Thus, I didn't initially want to work in an educational setting. Instead, my outspokenness and inquisitiveness sparked a passion for advocating for the unheard and challenging systemic inequities.

Fast forward, I found myself leaving the criminal justice field to pursue education and give voice to a population of young people disadvantaged in the criminal justice system that looked like me. I felt my calling was to give voice to the unheard, and inspire them to see the greatest in themselves. In education, I quickly emerged as a legal advocate, teacher, dean, and assistant principal, all in the public school setting, mostly in suburban Long Island, NY, districts.

My acceleration was initially encouraged, but after a glowing evaluation and multiple board and public recognitions, I was blocked from a promotion in another Long Island district and faced discrimination and microaggressions in my current district.

I was told I should be content with the fact that I was even in the position of leadership. My passion for helping others, pursuing terminal studies, and strong leadership agility was perceived as "too aggressive."

At the same time, I noticed that few women of color held executive superintendency in New York State public schools. As I dove into the literature, I soon learned this was not a "New York thing" but a United States issue, even while there was so little research on the matter. That baffled me. Even with cracks being made by White women and Black men as they broke into the superintendency pipeline, Black, indigenous, and people of color (BIPOC) women have made only marginal ripples in the glass ceiling of the superintendency pipeline. This phenomenon perplexed me for decades.

When I left America to pursue executive leadership aspirations abroad, seeking to escape the systemic microaggressions, gaslighting, and biases I had experienced, I soon came to realize that the educational executive leadership (superintendency in international schools) mirrored those same inequities and injustices. In the roles of head of school, consultant, and principal, I began to notice that the impact of Black women's marginalization on the executive level potentially perpetuated the inequities in curriculum, policy, enrollment, and recruitment of diverse staff. These relationships influence a passion to confront the lack of diversity and equity head on, both academically and professionally, in pursuit of justice.

Representation, to say the least, matters.

Serving as a head of school, principal, and consultant, I have seen firsthand how the absence of Black women in the field influenced my leadership style and focus on diversity, equity, inclusion, and justice (DEIJ) in education.

Having been on the receiving end of microaggressions and gaslighting, I can connect with the participants in this study. These experiences also impact attainment and retention in these executive superintendent and head roles. When the invisibility of certain groups is potentially linked to intersectionality "isms" such as racism and sexism, it becomes clear that understanding the factors associated with and behaviors influencing these disparities is also a social justice issue. Thus, my interest in this research is linked to my desire to improve the practices and policies that are causing the disparity and to draw attention to ways that injustices can be intentionally reformed to increase the number of Black women in the superintendency/headship. Moreover, I hope this study will influence and shape future research on why a more diverse group of leaders can be beneficial to students' learning and institution's success.

Like James Arthur Baldwin decades before me, the political unrest of the times and family brought me back stateside and fueled an urgency to address DEIJ and its lack in the educational system. To gain a deeper understanding, I immersed myself in various K–12 institutional types: parochial, public, international, and independent. Working closely with DEIJ practitioners, heads, and recruitment agencies, I gained firsthand insights into the issue, and my established relationships provided access to the associations from which I drew participants for this study. These personal experiences, coupled with my professional observations, ignited a curiosity that led me to question the systemic barriers faced by Black women in educational leadership and sparked my research journey. This book is the culmination of that journey, and it is my hope that it will inspire further dialogue.

Despite my personal connection to the topic, I was determined to approach this research with objectivity and rigor. The challenge I faced is that the study is near and dear to me, and I do not want to interject myself into the narratives of participants, no matter how similar they may seem. I employed the concepts of epoché and bracketing,[2] suspending my preconceived notions and judgments to allow the voices and experiences of the participants to emerge authentically. I also invited participants to review my interpretations of their responses to ensure accuracy and representation.

This research has been both enlightening and transformative, positively influencing how I lead and serve. It has reinforced my commitment to social justice in education and inspired me to use my voice and platform to advocate for change.

Clearly, research that claims absolution of any bias and subjectivity is flawed and questionable. Recognizing and acknowledging my connection to the subject is important and does not invalidate the significance of the study. Last, it is important that I talk about this research in a way that will affect future conversations and academic research. As Brunner stated, "Self-critique is a necessary step when seeking to significantly reduce research practices that restrict or limit discourse generation from typically marginalized groups of superintendents, superintendent candidates, and others."[3] I hope that this book will not only shed light on the challenges faced by Black women in educational leadership but also offer actionable strategies to dismantle those barriers.

Notes

1 Hurston, Z. N. (1942). *Dust tracks on a road*. Arno Press.
2 For more on these terms, see Creswell, J. W., & Poth, C. N. (2018). *Qualitative inquiry and research design* (4th ed.). Sage.
3 Brunner, C. C. (2008). Invisible, limited, and emerging discourse: Research practices that restrict and/or increase access for women and persons of color to the superintendency. *Journal of School Leadership*, *13*(4), 664.

ACKNOWLEDGMENTS

In pursuit of happiness and peace, I have navigated challenging obstacles and weathered severe storms. Amid it all, I am humbled to recognize God's unwavering power and love. He has bestowed upon me the greatest gifts, and through His teachings, I have gained the profound understanding that everything has its designated time and place, including a time to tear down and a time to build up.

The extraordinary Black women leaders who participated in this research inspire me tremendously. Exemplary is their commitment to making a substantial and meaningful difference in the lives of others. I fervently hope that this research, like their extraordinary contributions, will encourage people to persevere and keep moving forward, thereby inspiring positive change everywhere they go.

Throughout my doctoral journey, Dr. Eustace Thompson provided me with invaluable counsel, support, mentorship, and flexibility. His expertise and guidance have illuminated my path and have been a constant source of inspiration. The members of my dissertation committee, Drs. Rebecca Natow, Sean Fanelli, Tonie McDonald, and Marc Nivet, have my deepest gratitude. By consistently challenging me to my intellectual and professional limits, each of you has significantly contributed to my growth and development. Your insights, feedback, and assistance were indispensable to the creation of this work. Likewise, Dr. Mónica

Byrne-Jiménez, your commitment to diversity, education, and leadership inspired me to channel my own fervor, even in moments of discomfort, to promote awareness and development.

I would like to acknowledge Hofstra University for their support throughout my research journey. The resources and guidance provided by the institution were invaluable to the completion of this project.

To my publisher, Peter Lang, and the entire team, I extend my sincere gratitude for your belief in this project. In particular, I want to thank Dr. Alison Elizabeth Jefferson (Education Acquisitions Editor) for her unwavering support and guidance throughout the publishing process. Your dedication to bringing this book to fruition is deeply appreciated.

To Sonya Goode, my outstanding research analyst, and Dr. Julia, an exceptional editor, for their meticulous attention to detail, insightful comments, and commitment to ensuring the integrity and consistency of this work, they have been indispensable. Your expertise and dedication are deeply appreciated. I am also grateful to my talented niece, Sierra Wheeler, for her creative vision and skill in designing the beautiful book cover.

To my dear mother, Norma "Cherrie" Richards, an educator, social worker, mentor, and a genuine angel on this earth. You are the embodiment of grace, perseverance, and love—a guiding light through every storm. Your strength and wisdom have shaped me into the person I am today, and I am eternally grateful for your unwavering support.

And to my late father, Anthony "Prince" Richards (1942-2020), your tenacious spirit and unshakable belief in me continue to inspire me every day. Your legacy of speaking truth to power lives on through me, and I know you would be proud of this accomplishment.

To my brothers, Ewan and the late Omar Richards, you believed in my potential to become a lawyer, and while my path took a different turn, I hope you can see that my activism and passion still burn brightly.

Through this work, I continue to be a voice for the silenced, advocating for justice and equality. My family, friends, and mentors have been pillars of strength, celebrating every milestone and lifting me up during challenges. To my extended family, thank you for always being there to celebrate my triumphs and offer comfort during challenging times. As James Baldwin so eloquently stated, "Not everything that is faced can be changed, but nothing can be changed until it is faced." It is my hope that this research will contribute to facing the challenges in education leadership equity and result in positive change for future generations.

· 1 ·

UNMASKING THE INTERSECTION OF RACE AND GENDER IN TIMES OF SOCIAL UNREST

Ain't I a Woman?

—Sojourner Truth[1]

Since the public outrage of George Floyd and the racial endemic felt across the country, some in the literature and in this research have sensed a pullback or pullout of diversity, equity, and inclusion work. This has been particularly true since the conviction of Floyd's murderers. Moreover, there are the subtle undertone whispers that have lingered since—sentiments that society can go back to "normal" because justice was served, that schools are corrupting and promoting critical race theory in K–12 education, and that more women have arrived and succeeded in leadership.

The national attention paid to the challenges faced by antiracism and profeminist movements of Black males is quite fierce right now, to the point that it has all but eclipsed the discussion of challenges faced by Black women. Society has a tendency to recognize the antiracism movement as Black men and the feminist movement as white women, which has obscured the visibility of women of color in academia and social movements. Like a storm that can devour another, the intersection of race and gender frequently erases Black women from the discourse. Even with the social identity of women of color, Black women are frequently rendered invisible in comparison to women of other races. When viewed in this manner, the unique and intersecting challenges faced by Black women are consumed, diminished, and frequently overshadowed. This is why organizations like the African American Policy Forum (AAPF) and the Center for Intersectionality and Social Policy Studies (CISPS) have launched the #SayHerName campaign to draw attention to the stories and plights of victimized Black girls and women. In this context, the disregard for Black women opens up a larger conversation about inclusion, equity, and justice. Given that education is supposed to be the great equalizer, its essential to examine Black women in educational leadership roles, such as school superintendents and head of schools.

There has been very little research on the experiences of Black women in the educational superintendency. Amie B. Revere was one of the pioneers who offered an extensive look at the Black female superintendent.[2] Revere's sampling and findings may still be the most comprehensive published study describing Black women superintendents.[3] Revere provided comprehensive insight into the historical profile of these women. Other published works on the subject[4] have not been able to capture a complete list of Black women superintendents in the United States.

Some vital scholars[5] have raised concerns about the limited, missing, and aggregated data on women and people of color in the superintendency. Within the scope of research and discourse, the choice about which and how much data to publish can result in the reinforcement of the status quo. If data are conveniently inaccessible or there has been intentional nonreporting, researchers must raise the question of limited accessibility of data by gender, race, and the combination of both.

Limited research and data misinterpretation can cause harm that further marginalizes Black women superintendents. Research that does not consider multiple perspectives when interpreting results risks being misleading and/or erroneous. Data analysis should be a layered process that begins with and intersects between various connected impact points.

Brunner[6] argued that the shared understanding and dominant discourse on the ideal superintendent and the trajectory (career path) to the superintendency leans heavily to support the positionality and power of White males and excludes women and persons of color. Research has identified common attributes and backgrounds for superintendents, such as prior service, which grossly favors White males and excludes women and persons of color.

Researchers can generate new discourse that changes the landscape of the superintendency. We have a compelling responsibility and power to examine, shape, and disseminate collective knowledge about the superintendency that provides a context to purposefully disrupt White male dominance and positionality in the field. Black women are physically underrepresented in the superintendency role, yet there has been so little research giving voice to their plight and experiences.

Shaping An Inclusive Future: Black Women in Education Leadership

The marginalization that operates within the educational system is a microcosm of the institutionalized discourses that legitimize the extant power relations in the structure and law of our society.[7] Therefore, if education is to be the key to expanding perspectives and creating hope and opportunity, then antiracism and antifeminism must be dismantled and disrupted first within the context of educational institutions. For this reason, it is essential to recognize the significance of the demarginalization of Black women in educational leadership for the advancement of humanity as a whole.

Researchers have extensively documented how a person's ability to access the superintendency depends on their race or gender. What remains unreported, consciously or unconsciously, is how the combination of race and gender further restricts access than the single axis of each identifier separately. In fact, the existing power relations between those who hold the power to report data chose to report the points of view of White men, while allowing their representation and existence to overwhelm the only perspective truth.[8] Further, the decision to exclude the voices of women and people of color has made the discourse of the minority population, particularly those with intersecting identities, essentially invisible and missing in action[9] in the executive leadership field in nearly all industries.

It's crucial to demarginalize Black women in educational leadership for a number of reasons. First of all, it encourages equitable representation and diversity in positions of leadership in education. We know that even though 65% of the teachers in the United States are women, only 13.2% of the superintendents are women.[10] The significant underrepresentation of Black women as superintendents and heads of schools, despite their presence in the teaching profession, perpetuates systemic inequalities and denies them the opportunity to contribute their unique perspectives and experiences. Increasing their presence in leadership positions not only enhances representation but also fosters a more inclusive and culturally responsive educational environment.

Second, elevating Black women educators into leadership positions serves as a powerful model for all students, especially Black girls, who can envision themselves in inspiring positions of authority and aspire to similar roles.[11] Representation matters, as it positively influences the academic and social-emotional development of students. By dismantling systemic barriers and providing equitable pathways to leadership, educational institutions can cultivate a new generation of empowered and inspired students. As these women shatter glass ceilings and overcome concrete barriers, they forge new paths, becoming leaders who shape a brighter future for humanity.

The inclusion of Black women in educational leadership introduces diverse perspectives, ideas, and approaches to the decision-making process. Their unique lived experience, shaped by intersecting racial and gender identities, offer valuable insights that can inform policies and practices designed to address systemic inequities and improve outcomes for marginalized students. When diverse perspectives are represented at the leadership table, educational institutions can develop more comprehensive and effective strategies to promote equity, dismantle biases, and create inclusive learning environments. Then, schools can truly foster a sense of belonging in their communities.

Demarginalizing Black women in educational leadership also challenges and disrupts long-standing stereotypes and biases that impede advancement.[12] It requires a commitment to dismantling systemic barriers and nurturing a culture of inclusion, equity, innovation, and equal opportunity. By actively working to eliminate these barriers, educational institutions can foster an ecosystem that values and supports professional development. Ensuring the voices of Black women are invited, respected, and influential in educational policies and practices can only contribute to a bright future.

Black women in educational leadership are essential for achieving equity, promoting diversity, challenging stereotypes, and cultivating inclusive learning environments. By recognizing and addressing the obstacles that hinder their full access and participation, educational institutions can unlock transformative change within the education system.

Notes

1 Former slave Sojourner Truth's (1797–1883) "Ain't I a Woman?" speech was given at an Ohio Women's Convention in 1851.

2 Revere, A. B. (1987). Black women superintendents in the United States: 1984–1985. *Journal of Negro Education*, 56(4), 510–520.

3 Brunner, C. C., & Peyton-Caire, L. (2000). Seeking representation supporting Black female graduate students who aspire to the superintendency. *Urban Education*, *35*(5), 532–548; Jackson, B. L. (1999). Getting inside history—against all odds: African-American women school superintendents. In C. C. Brunner (Ed.), *Sacred dreams: Women in the superintendency* (pp. 141–160). State University of New York.

4 Alston, J. A. (1999). Climbing hills and mountains: Black women making it to the superintendency. In C. C. Brunner (Ed.), *Sacred dreams: Women and the superintendency* (pp. 79–90). State University of New York; Brunner & Peyton-Caire, 2000; Jackson, 1999; Tillman, B. A., & Cochran, L. L. (2000). Desegregating urban school administration: A pursuit of equity for Black women superintendents. *Education and Urban Society*, *33*(1), 44–59.

5 Alston, 1999; Alston, J. A. (2000). Missing from action: Where are the Black female school superintendents? *Urban Education*, *35*(5), 525–531; Brunner, 2008; Jackson, 1999; Jackson, J., & Shakeshaft, C. (2003, April 22). *The pool of African-American candidates for the superintendency* [Paper presentation]. American Education Research Association Annual Meeting, Chicago, IL, United States. https://files.eric.ed.gov/fulltext/ED479479.pdf; Revere, 1987.

6 Brunner, C. C. (2008). Invisible, limited, and emerging discourse: Research practices that restrict and/or increase access for women and persons of color to the superintendency. *Journal of School Leadership*, *13*(4), 428–450. https://doi.org/10.1177/105268460301300405.

7 Crenshaw, K. (1991). Mapping the margins: Intersectionality, identity politics, and violence against women of color. Stanford Law Review, 43(6), 1241–1299.

8 Brunner, 2008.

9 Alston, J. A. (2000). Missing from action: Where are the Black female school superintendents? *Urban Education*, *35*(5), 525–531.

10 Alston, J. A. (1999). Climbing hills and mountains: Black women making it to the superintendency. In C. C. Brunner (Ed.), *Sacred dreams: Women and the superintendency* (pp. 79–90). State University of New York.

11 Alston, J. A. (1999). Climbing hills and mountains: Black women making it to the superintendency. In C. C. Brunner (Ed.), *Sacred dreams: Women and the superintendency* (pp. 79–90). State University of New York.

12 Alston, J. A. (1999). Climbing hills and mountains: Black women making it to the superintendency. In C. C. Brunner (Ed.), *Sacred dreams: Women and the superintendency* (pp. 79–90). State University of New York.

· 2 ·

WOMEN AND PERSONS OF COLOR IN EDUCATIONAL LEADERSHIP

All the Women Are White, All the Blacks Are Men, but Some of Us Are Brave

—Gloria T. Hull, Patricia Bell Scott, and Barbara Smith (Eds.)[1]

Historically, White males have dominated the field of educational leadership. In fact, the 2000 U.S. Census Bureau identified the public school superintendent position the most male-dominated executive leadership position in the United States.

In 2007, the American Association of School Administrators (AASA) reported White male school leadership at 70%.[2] The AASA survey of public school superintendents reported the role as disproportionately male and overwhelmingly White. An overwhelming percentage of public schools, over 93%, were led by White males.

All this has been happening even as women greatly outnumber men as classroom teachers. Scholars[3] have examined White males' continuing dominance in the industry. Such debates have brought attention to the absence of females in the superintendency pipeline, and some progress has been made in terms of women gaining superintendent positions in American public schools.[4] However, these cracks in the glass ceiling have almost exclusively benefited the privileged female gender of White women.

At the turn of the millennium, less than 50 of the approximately 14,500 superintendents in the United States, were Black women, accounting for less than 1% of all superintendents.[5] Additionally, these Black women earned lower salaries than their counterparts. Similarly, in 2004, out of 15,000 superintendents across the United States, the National Alliance for Black School Educators reported that only 114 were Black women. These statistics highlight the severe underrepresentation of Black women in the superintendent roles, both in practice and academic research.

Black women continue to have limited access to and involvement in school leadership at the executive superintendent and head level. Scholars have begun to unearth these inequities, noting that women of color remain one of the most neglected subjects in educational leadership practice and research. To address this, we must first understand why and acknowledge the social constructs that contribute to this disparity.

Intersectionality, a concept introduced by Kimberlé Crenshaw,[6] offers a framework for examining this phenomenon. She explained that "the experiences Black women face are not subsumed within the traditional boundaries of race or gender discrimination... [They] cannot be captured wholly by looking at... the dimensions of the experiences separately."[7] Few scholars have looked at the intersecting identities of Black women and sought to understand their voices, their experiences, and the structural factors that influence their underrepresentation in school superintendency and headships.

The voices, perspectives, stories, and journeys of these women must be heard to understand the disparities that exist. The AASA put out a study of U.S. public school superintendents that looked at their work over 10 years.[8] It showed that the need for more research is influenced by three important factors. First, minority respondents reported that they encountered discrimination in their trajectory toward the superintendency. Second, while the proportion of White women superintendents has significantly increased, reaching 9% in 2010, the number of Black women superintendents has decreased. The percentage of women (of any race) superintendents remained below 10% until the 1990s, when it doubled from 6.6% to 13.2%.[9] Third and most striking, the AASA survey revealed that more than half of the BIPOC respondents stated that they planned to leave the superintendency by 2015. This highlights the issues of fatigue, retention, and exhaustion that those Black women who do make it into the superintendency or headship face, often leading to their rapid exit from the field.[10]

While there has been a notable increase in Black male and White female representation in the superintendency, Black women remain underrepresented; creating inequities in K–12 superintendency.

According to Revere,[11] from 1984 to 1985, of the 16,000 U.S. school districts, there were only 29 Black female superintendents. Revere's 1987 cohort was the total population of Black female superintendents in the United States, of which 22 (75.8%) participated. The sampling context represented participants from suburban, urban, and rural locations. The enrollment sizes of districts ranged from 300 to 88,700, mirroring the diversity of the locations.

Revere conducted personal interviews with Black female superintendents in the states of Alabama, California, Georgia, Illinois, Minnesota, Mississippi, New Jersey, New York, Ohio, Virginia and the District of Columbia. The findings offer demographic descriptions of the superintendents and their perspectives in relation to their roles.

Jackson[12] sought to update Revere's data in 1999 and assessed the number of Black female superintendents as 33 in 1993–1994. Jackson was able to interview 41 total respondents which included current and former Black female superintendents.

In both studies, the profiles of the Black superintendents revealed the following themes: family support, preparedness, location, context, and culture. Of these, family support and structure played the greatest role in nurturing leadership development for the superintendency and the superintendents' success in the role once appointed.

The Black women superintendents were influenced by their fathers and participated in pageants, public speaking, and church events that helped them to develop leadership skills. Revere found that most participants (63.6%) gained their superintendencies when they were 46 years old or older; some were even onto their second superintendency. Additionally, the same number were married, and that 80% of the participants had children.

The context, circumstance, and location in which these women gained superintendencies were interesting. Revere found that the women's district size and location varied. Approximately 91% (20 participants) led were districts composed of elementary and secondary schools, and of these, 16 participants (72.8%) were city superintendents. While Black female superintendents did not work only in minority communities, the majority did. Black superintendents were often hired to lead "leftovers" districts that White superintendents no longer wanted—those that had "fallen into disrepair,"[13] or those with severe financial problems that needed to be fixed.

Revere attributed these women's success to six factors. First, they demonstrated competence, characterized by high energy, strong public relations, and good organizational skills. Second, they were industrious, hard-working, and resourceful women. Third, these women had strong self-esteem. Fourth, these women persevered despite the demands of the job. Fifth, they were aware of their interpersonal, humanistic, and motivational skills. The women also knew how to exert authority and enhance their power base. Last, the participants' willingness to relocate was instrumental to their obtaining their superintendency.

While Jackson's study was a decade later, she also encountered data-collection issues. Jackson asserted that there was no organization or source compiling accurate and complete information on women, much less Black women superintendents. She warned that without this information, equity progress cannot be appropriately measured or tracked.

Additionally, issues of why and how so few Black females are in the U.S. educational superintendency have not truly been addressed in the literature, thus there is little to help us understand these women's situations, challenges, and strengths, information vital to decreasing the marginalization of Black females at the highest levels of U.S. educational institutions.

The underrepresentation of Black women in educational leadership is a significant issue that warrants further investigation and action to address systemic barriers and promote equity in leadership opportunities.

The purpose of this book is to shed light on and foster a deeper understanding of the lived experiences of Black women superintendents and heads of school in the United States. Drawing upon my familiarity with the New York State educational districts, I delve into these women's experiences in their leadership roles, the barriers they faced in their trajectory, and the impact these experiences have had on their leadership styles.

Researchers' decisions to bring attention to and publish data about the superintendent pipeline "can result in the reification of the status quo and/or the generation of a tremendously powerful new discourse that establishes the inclusive norms for a new genre of superintendency."[14] The latter is my hope here: to provide a better understanding of the causes influencing this historical trend. Further, I want to help researchers in the field identify ways to reform the pipeline so it is more inclusive for aspiring Black women superintendents.

My concerns gravitated toward two major issues: the challenges and supports Black women superintendents and heads have encountered in leading their schools, and these women's perceptions on how they feel the superintendent/headship pipeline can be more inclusive for Black women.

Centering and Amplifying Black Women Superintendents' and Heads' Voices

For decades, the voices and experiences of Black women in educational leadership have been ignored, understudied, and unheard. Dominant narratives, often shaped by White men, White women, and even Black men, have frequently overshadowed the perspectives of Black female leaders. Yet, it is essential to recognize the immense importance of amplifying these marginalized voices. By simply allowing Black women to speak their authentic voices, unburdened by the expectations or interpretations of others, we unlock a wealth of untapped knowledge and essential truths.

Providing platforms for Black women's voices in the context of superintendency allows them to share their experiences and contributes to a broader understanding of educational leadership. Their unique perspectives and lived experiences offer new epistemologies and knowledge systems that challenge and expand upon existing paradigms. By delving into "herstory," we unveil hidden narratives, spotlight neglected issues, and illuminate the nuanced complexities of the Black women's educational leadership experiences.

Moreover, providing Black women with the opportunity to share their stories and perspectives not only promotes dignity but also enriches our understanding of their lived experiences. It recognizes their agency, resilience, and contributions, affirming their rightful place as leaders and pioneers of change. Through these narratives, we can rewrite and reconstruct history, fostering a more inclusive and accurate understanding of the challenges, victories, and contributions of Black women in educational leadership. By acknowledging and honoring their voices, we pave the way for a new history that recognizes the multiplicity of experiences and cultivates a more equitable and just educational system.

Ultimately, centering the perspectives of Black women in superintendency enables a more comprehensive understanding of educational leadership. Their stories hold transformative power, not only in terms of individual but also collective empowerment reshaping educational systems to be more inclusive, equitable, and reflective of diverse perspectives. It is our responsibility as scholars and educators to actively seek out, listen to, and amplify the voices of those marginalized like Black women, ensuring that their narratives are heard and valued. By doing so, we promote social justice, and cultivate an educational landscape that is more inclusive for all.

Black Feminist Thought and Intersectionality Theoretical Frameworks

I employed two interconnected Afrocentric theoretical lenses: Black feminist thought and intersectionality. The Black feminist thought argues that Black women have two levels of knowledge that offer a unique set of understandings because there is a "double consciousness" of being both Black and female.[15] This perspectives challenges the dominance of androcentrism and ethnocentric viewpoints, which often marginalize the experiences of Black women.

White males are identified as doubly privileged within societal and school leadership hierarchies due to their race and gender. While Black men face racial marginalizaton, they still benefit from male privilege in a patriarchal androcentric society. Similarly, White women experience gender-based marginalization hold racial privilege in a predominated White society.

Crenshaw critiques single-axis frameworks, such as antiracist and feminist theories; further perpetuate discriminatory consequences because they treat race and gender as mutually exclusive categories, failing to recognize the intersectional nature of discrimination faced by Black women. Intersectionality is presented as a more comprehensive framework for examining the hierarchical disparities and muti-layered disadvantages experienced by Black women.[16] Figure 1 illustrates the hierarchical structure and level that the combination of race and gender plays in society.

The illustration demonstrates how the double consciousness (i.e., double jeopardy) of Black women falls into the societal hierarchical structure. They

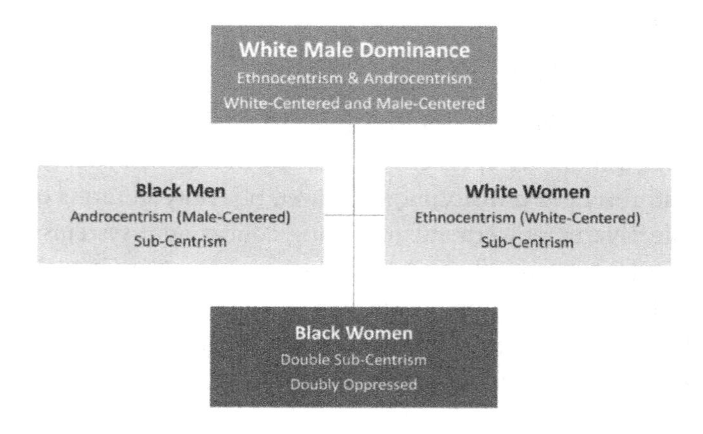

Figure 1 *Intersectionality: The Hierarchy of Social Constructs of Race and Gender*

are marginalized for both their gender and their race. Black feminist thought suggests that researchers should capture the unique experiences of those doubly marginalized by race and gender.

In Chapter 1, my research highlights how societal forces have obscured the visibility of women of color within the antiracist and feminist movements. Black women, in particular, often experience erasure and face invisibility even within the broader category of women of color. It is important to acknowledge that women from diverse racial and ethnic backgrounds, such as Latina, Indigenous, and Asian women, also face exclusion from educational leadership positions, including superintendencies and school heads. While this study primarily focuses on the experiences of Black women, it acknowledges the intersecting experiences of other women of color. However, exploring the experiences of these groups falls beyond the scope of this research, and it is critical that future research undertakes this area of inquiry. This study aims to advocate for greater inclusion of underrepresented and marginalized groups in education leadership, recognizing that society as a whole benefits when these groups gain access and visibility.[17]

Intersectionality, rooted in Black feminism, essentially argues that the synthesis of multiple oppressive identities is more oppressive than a single one. Intersectionality is an analytical tool for examining and exposing the social context in which people with intertwined oppressive identities have completely different experiences from those of people with only one of those oppressive identities.

Black female superintendents and heads of schools possess unique perspectives of both womanhood and race that manifest differently for White women and Black men, who are also marginalized in the executive superintendency role. In fact, Crenshaw[18] argues that the intersecting dynamics of these two oppressive identities create a qualitatively different experience for women of color. This distinct form of oppression, often ignored by the courts and the literature, contributes to the further disempowerment and polarization of Black women.

Intersectionality, a powerful tool for analysis, has been applied to diverse areas such as the law (domestic violence and rape cases), sex orientation, and disabilities (e.g., girls with autism). While feminism and racism are recognized as marginalizing factors in school superintendencies, the combined impact of being Black and female have essentially gone unnoticed, as evidenced by the lack of respresentation of Black women superintendents'(heads') in research and practice. The multidimensional and intertwining experiences of Black women superintendents are theoretically erased when their experiences are only analyzed through the lens of race or gender.

Intersectionality is not merely a framework that recognizes the intersecting oppressive identities people experience; it is a practical tool applicable across varied disciplines. It provides insights into advocating for inclusivity, addresses power structures that affect Black women, and transcends abstract theory to inform social reform, with potential for global application. As Carbado et al. note, intersectionality is not something that can be confined. Instead, it can be a starting point for social movement and change. Ultimately, the goal of intersectionality is "not simply to understand social relations of power... but to bring the often hidden dynamics forward in order to transform them."[19]

Knowledge and experience cannot be evaluated independently of their social and historical contexts. Rather, researchers must employ epistemological diversity to limit single-mindedness and to expose controversies or new truths. The marginalization of Black women in the superintendency and their limited visibility in the research frame the conceptual framework for this book. To capture the essence of Black women's experiences fully, an Afrocentric epistemology is needed to fully grasp Black women's way of knowing. Intersectionality is an Afrocentric epistemology "for contextualizing the epistemological worldview of people [who] have experienced racism, discrimination, and marginalization."[20] Thus, I gathered the perspectives of Black female superintendents/heads, utilizing Afrocentric epistemologies, such as Black feminist theory, Chica feminist ideology,[21] and intersectionality. New research discourse is needed that supports equitable and inclusive leadership models that "compels women and persons of color to aspire to roles like the superintendency [and headship]... [and this discourse] must be visible, unlimited, and considered foundational emerging research."[22]

The conceptual framework presented in Figure 2 is designed to guide research that intentionally examined the unique lived experiences and leadership of Black women superintendents/heads in the hope of uncovering new truths and perspectives that could help to make the pipeline more inclusive in the future. It was structured in a hierarchical format, with each level building upon the foundation of the previous. Identity, that is the intersectionality of race and gender, is the foundation. The historiography of the superintendency and headship, the second level, focuses on the historical, political, and social context of educational institutions and leadership roles. This level aims to highlight the factors and experiences that shaped these Black women leaders. The third level centers on the emerging discourse that aims to increase understanding and access. The final level explore how Black women lead—their influence, impact and inclusivity shape or inform outcomes that shift the paradigm.

The top echelons of public and independent schools remain overwhelmingly devoid of Black women leaders. In terms of the acquisition of school superintendencies, there is a pressing need to address the inequities and disparities in educational leadership, practice, and policy, as there have been decades without any appreciable changes in the inclusion of Black women in the superintendency and head-of-school pipelines. When data are not broken down or made public, their voices are rendered invisible. Overall, this conceptual guide provides an approach to investigating these women' complex experiences, and aims to generate new knowledge that can promote meaningful change in the educational pipeline and landscape.

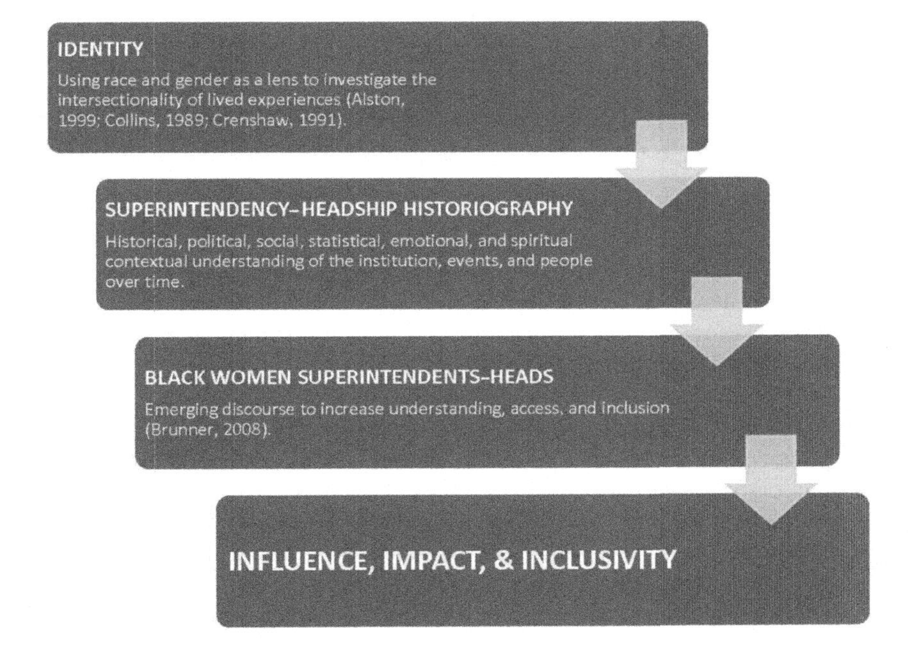

Figure 2 *Conceptual Framework*

The predicament of Black women in leadership was starkly illuminated on the international stage during Ketanji Brown Jackson's U.S. Supreme Court Senate confirmation hearings. Despite her impeccable, credentials and record, Justice Jackson endured heightened scrutiny compared to other nominees, revealing biases rooted in her race, gender, and political affiliation. A similar scenario unfolded more recently when Dr. Claudine Gay, Harvard University's first Black woman president, faced pressure and was forced to resign prematurely. These incidents serve as a potent reminder of the persistent challenges faced by Black women at the intersection of race, gender and power. These instances underscore the deeply ingrained biases and microaggressions that continue to hinder their advancement, revealing the urgent need to dismantle systemic barriers and create more equitable pathways to leadership. As Wiley et al. eloquently stated, "through the accounts of other women educators, aspiring leaders might reflect on their own individual journeys and benefit from the experiences of others as they seek leadership positions in public education."[23] In alignment with Black feminist thought and intersectionality, the data, findings and theories in this book offer crucial insights that inform educational practices, research, policy, and leadership development.

Notes

1 Hull, A. (Ed.), Scott, P. B. (Ed.), & Smith, B. (Ed.). (1982). *But some of us are brave: All the women are White, all the Blacks are men: Black women's studies*. The Feminist Press at CUNY.

2 Glass, T. E., & Franceschini, L. A. (2007). *The state of the American school superintendency: A mid-decade study*. American Association of School Administrators.

3 Alston, J. A. (2005). Tempered radicals and servant leaders: Black females persevering in the superintendency. *Educational Administration Quarterly, 41*(4), 675–688; Brown, A. R. (2014). The recruitment and retention of African American women as public school superintendents. *Journal of Black Studies, 45*(6), 573–593. https://doi.org/10.1177/0021934714542157.

4 Brunner & Peyton-Caire, 2000; Glass, T. E. (1992). *The 1992 study of the American superintendency: American's education leaders in a time of reform*. American Association of School Administrators; Shakeshaft, C. (1989). *Women in education administration*. Sage.

5 Brunner & Peyton-Caire, 2000; Jackson, B. L. (1999). Getting inside history—against all odds: African-American women school superintendents. In C. C. Brunner (Ed.), *Sacred dreams: Women in the superintendency* (pp. 141–160). State University of New York.

6 Crenshaw explained how Black women are marginalized both within White patriarchal society and within feminist and antiracist theories. Crenshaw, K. (1989). Demarginalizing the intersection of race and sex: A Black feminist critique of antidiscrimination doctrine, feminist theory and antiracist politics. *University of Chicago Legal Forum, 1989*(1).

7 Crenshaw, 1991.

8 Kowalski, T. J., McCord, R. S., Pretson, G. J., Young, P. I., & Ellerson, N. M. (2011). *The American school superintendent: 2010 decennial study*. Rowman & Littlefield/American Association of School Superintendents (AASA).

9 Björk, L. (2000). Introduction: Women in the superintendency—advances in research and theory. *Educational Administration Quarterly*, *36*(1), 5–17.
10 Jackson, 1999.
11 Revere, A. B. (1986). *A description of Black female school superintendents. The Black superintendency: Challenge or crisis?* Symposium conducted at the meeting of the American Educational Research Association of San Francisco, CA; Revere, 1987.
12 Jackson, B. L. (1999). Getting inside history—against all odds: African-American women school superintendents. In C. C. Brunner (Ed.), *Sacred dreams: Women in the superintendency* (pp. 141–160). State University of New York.
13 Jackson, J., & Shakeshaft, C. (2003, April 22). *The pool of African-American candidates for the superintendency* [Paper presentation]. American Education Research Association Annual Meeting, Chicago, IL, United States. https://files.eric.ed.gov/fulltext/ED479479.pdf, p. 14.
14 Brunner, C. C. (2008). Invisible, limited, and emerging discourse: Research practices that restrict and/or increase access for women and persons of color to the superintendency. *Journal of School Leadership*, *13*(4), 428–450. https://doi.org/10.1177/105268460301300405, p. 661.
15 Collins, P. H. (1989). The social construction of Black feminist thought. *Signs*, *14*(4), 745–773. http://www.jstor.org/stable/3174683.
16 Crenshaw, K. (1989). Demarginalizing the intersection of race and sex: A Black feminist critique of antidiscrimination doctrine, feminist theory and antiracist politics. *University of Chicago Legal Forum*, *1989*(1).
17 Crenshaw, K. (1989). Demarginalizing the intersection of race and sex: A Black feminist critique of antidiscrimination doctrine, feminist theory and antiracist politics. *University of Chicago Legal Forum*, *1989*(1).
18 Crenshaw, 1989.
19 Carbado, D. W., Crenshaw, K. W., Mays, V. M., & Tomlinson, B. (2013). Intersectionality: Mapping the movements of a theory. *Du Bois Review*, *10*(2), 303–312. https://doi.org/10.1017/S1742058X13000349, p. 312.
20 Ladson-Billings, 2000, as cited in Jean-Marie, G., Williams, V. A., & Sherman, S. L. (2009). Black women's leadership experiences: Examining the intersectionality of race and gender. *Advances in Developing Human Resources*, *11*(5), 562–581. https://doi.org/10.1177/1523422309351836.
21 For more on this, see Rodriguez, S. A. (2014). *Extraordinary women in Texas: A phenomenological study of Mexican American female superintendents* [Doctoral dissertation, Texas State University].
22 Brunner, C. C. (2008). Invisible, limited, and emerging discourse: Research practices that restrict and/or increase access for women and persons of color to the superintendency. *Journal of School Leadership*, *13*(4), 428–450. https://doi.org/10.1177/105268460301300405, p. 678.
23 Wiley et al., 2017, p. 19.

· 3 ·

THEORY-BUILDING CASE STUDIES: ILLUMINATING HIDDEN VOICES

Research is formalized curiosity. It is poking and prying with a purpose.

—Zora Neale Hurston[1]

Due to the scarcity of empirical data on Black women in leadership positions, theory-building, rather than theory-testing, is warranted in this study. My purpose was to gain an understanding of an often-unexplored phenomenon by using case studies to explore and enhance the ideas and functions of intersectionality theory. Because case study theory-building is not a widely used research design and focuses on interpreting meaning through social actors, extra care was employed.

> It is helpful to preempt misunderstanding by engaging in systematic data collection and theory development processes that are reported with transparent description, particularly regarding how the theory was inducted from data… The key is to convey [the] rigor, creativity, and open-mindedness of the research processes while sidestepping confusion and philosophical pitfalls.[2]

Clearly, case-study research can be used to develop theories, but it is not inherently a theory-building methodology. Because this research was tightly scoped within the extant theory of intersectionality, utilizing qualitative theory-building case studies, I looked to Eisenhardt's[3] methodological process as a guide. The process includes developing the research question; using theoretically specified sampling; incorporating multiple data-collection methods (qualitative and quantitative), conducting cross-case analysis; examining relationships to shape hypotheses that confirm, extend, or sharpen theory; comparing them with the literature; and reaching theoretical saturation when possible. The goal of theory-building case studies like this one is not to model real-world phenomena, but to understand real-world phenomena in the context of the case (see Figure 3).

An intrinsic case study illustrates the shared experience within the context of the issue being explored. A case-study approach focuses on the unique circumstances of the case itself resembling narrative research while still holding true to the analytical procedures of case-study inquiry. As such, I constructed the research questions explored here in a general fashion to allow participants' experiences to provoke new theories or refine existing ones.

Noting that internal generalization is a key issue and validity threat for qualitative case-study research, I purposefully infused variation into the sampling pool of Black women superintendents by including eligible participants in both public and independent school settings. Through this research, I

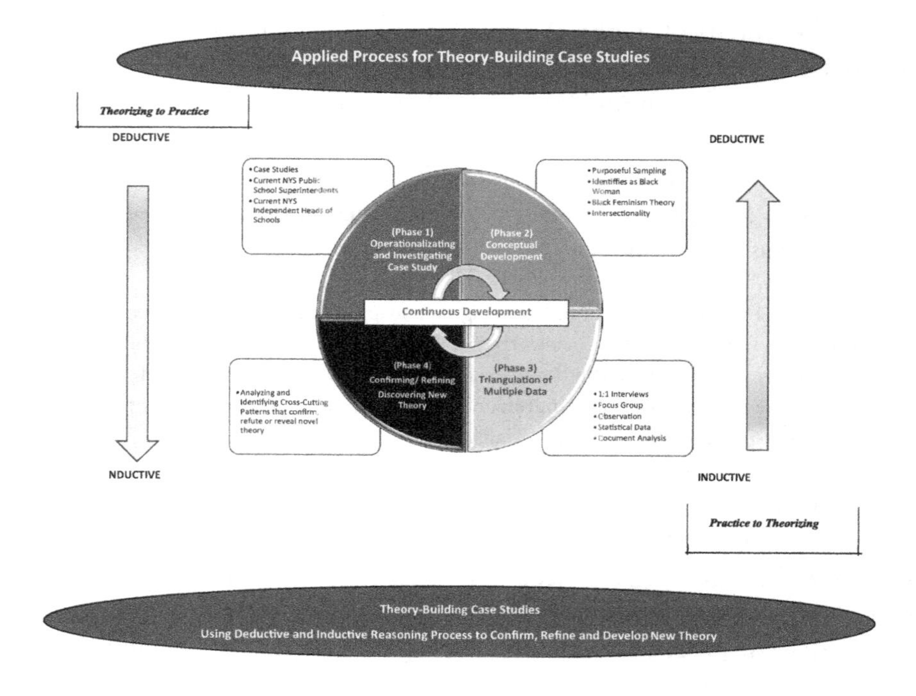

Figure 3 *Applied Roles of Analysis for Case Study Theory-Building*

sought to identify causal explanations and reform the inequities that exist in the K–12 executive leadership pipeline.

According to the National Alliance of Black School Educators, the Eastern region of the United States had the highest percentage of Black superintendents in 2013. For this reason, this study's field setting was based in the Eastern region, more specifically, New York State.

The field setting for this study included K–12 schools throughout New York State, excluding New York City public schools due to their structural differences from the average New York State public and independent schools. Data, including interviews, focus groups, and document analysis, were gathered. Most of these were virtually collected via Zoom. Participants for this study were solicited through education leadership networks and associations such as the New York State Council of School Superintendents (NYSCOSS) and the National Association of Independent Schools (NAIS).

In the end, six Black women who were heads or superintendents of schools in New York State agreed to be interviewed, sharing their lived experiences. Given the limited number of Black women in these roles within the United States and in the New York State region, I omitted identifiable district demographics and details to protect the these participants' anonymity. Recognizing that their experiences likely differed from those of the dominant group (Whites and male), I found their perspectives provided an interpretive lens through which calls for reform emerged.

I used a semi-structured interview protocol,[4] allowing some unstructured and unelicited responses. Four participants participated in one-on-one interviews (via Zoom) that lasted 45 minutes to an hour. I asked open-ended questions, such as, "If you could write a prelude to your memoirs/story of your life as a superintendent, what would it say?" I encouraged them to elaborate on the details of their experience without interruption. The interview protocol included main, follow-up, and probing questions to ensure sufficient detail and to draw a convincing case.

The participants in one-on-one interviews were also invited to participate in a synchronous focus group via Zoom. The focus group panel consisted of three participants: one who also participated in a one-on-one interview, and two others who participated in the focus panel only. The focus group interview offered insights into participants individually and their reactions to one another. This helped to formulate the context of the inquiry for the participants, while inviting participants to be open about their personal experience as it related to the research questions. Before meeting for the focus group, participants signed a confidentiality statement in a show of good faith. While a semi-structured interview protocol was used, the participants engaged in continued dialogue that built upon each other's responses, allowing many unstructured and unelicited responses.

As the moderator, I established guidelines, norms, and confidentiality expectations to encourage all voices, foster open communication, active listening and discourage judgmental dispositions and groupthink.[5] I purposefully facilitated a safe space for participants to share their perceptions, ensuring they felt comfortable and unintimidated through both verbal and nonverbal cues. The introductory questions were designed to build rapport within the group, spark their interests, and encourage interactions that would nurture positive group dynamics.[6]

In addition to interviews and a focus group, document analysis was employed.[7] The data collected included job descriptions, resumes, and quantifiable leadership survey data, allowing descriptive statistics to enhance the qualitative analysis through triangulation. In my document analysis, I identified, appraised, and synthesized the data into meaningful themes to enhance credibility and reduce bias.

An ongoing discussion about hiring biases in leadership emerged from the interview, focus group, and quantitative data. To further investigate this, I added an observation protocol and attended two workshops on recruitment and identifying implicit biases. These observations, focusing on the presenter and attendees (who included board members and heads of color), served as an additional qualitative tool within the naturalistic case-study design setting. These observations offered the opportunity to notice things about the participants' experiences and interactions that may appear routine to those experiencing it. As I was a member of the audience, I did not disclose my role as an observer, and these sessions were not recorded. These unobtrusive observations offered a unique vantage point into established routines, research-based practices in action, and the influence of the gatekeepers within the leadership culture of this case study.

Document archival and observation notes provided evidence to confirm, contrast, and reshape the understanding of the "why" behind the phenomenon I was studying. This triangulation increased the study's validity, answered descriptive research questions, and facilitated theory-building within the context of the case.

Case-study research served as a method of theory-building and a strategy for integrating multiple methods to understand how intersectionality influenced Black women's lived experiences in the superintendent and head roles. In the first cycle, I used line-by-line open coding and employed both inductive and deductive methods. Initially codes emerged inductively from the data in the interview transcripts. These data were then deductively categorized around the study's research questions. I used NVivo version 12 Pro coding software to manage, organize, and analyze the data.

In the second cycle, an additional independent investigator analyzed specifically coded interview transcripts, separate from my own analysis. Eisenhardt explained why using additional investigators helps the researcher build a case-study theory in two ways.

> First they enhance the creative potential of the study… [They] often have complementary insights which add to the richness of the data, and their different perspectives increase the likelihood of capitalizing on any novel insights which may be in the data. Second, the convergence of observations from multiple investigators enhances confidence in the findings… while conflicting perceptions keep the group from premature closure. Thus, the use of more investigators builds confidence in the findings and increases the likelihood of surprising findings.[8]

Using the independent analyst strengthened the reflective analysis and enhanced validity, ensuring my potential biases did not influence my initial conclusions.[9]

During the second cycle, I divided the data by source and used a coding analysis spreadsheet to organize within-case and a cross-case analysis. Analytic memoing helped to summarize the data into smaller concepts and patterns, while axial coding was used to analyze emerging patterns. Axial coding is inferential and offers a broader perspective that is more focused, helping the researcher surface deeper cross-case understandings of casual constructs and develop theoretical constructs.[10] The patterns were initially structured around the intersectionality framework and the research questions, but they were not confined to these.

As I recognized intersecting patterns emerge in the data, selective and storyline coding allowed analysis and conceptualization of participants' narratives around core categories, systemically reconstructing themes based on the intersectionality framework. These emergent themes became theoretical arguments arising from the "*pattern-match* between theory and data."[11] Through the triangulation of multiple data sources (observations, data, documents), I applied aspects of theory-building to refine and modify the understanding of intersectionality viewing it not just as a theoretical framework but also as a method and tool.

Table 1 *Addressing Threats to Validity and Reliability*

Threat to Validity/ Reliability	Steps Taken to Address Threat
Researcher Bias	Researcher Perspective: Reflected on potential biases, employing bracketing techniques (Creswell & Poth, 2018).
	Purposeful Sampling: Selected diverse, knowledgeable participants to mitigate bias (Eisenhardt & Graebner, 2007).
	Independent Research Analyst: Utilized an independent analyst for a fresh perspective and increased confidence in findings.
Reactivity	Researcher Perspective: Acknowledged potential influence and used it as a tool to inform the research process.
	Triangulation: Employed multiple data sources to cross-validate insights (Maxwell, 2013; Natow, 2020).
	Member Checking: Participants reviewed transcripts to ensure their voices were accurately represented.
Internal Generalizability	Diversity: Purposeful sampling included Black women superintendents from diverse school settings.
	Mixed Data Sources: Combined qualitative data with descriptive analysis to strengthen insights (Creswell & Poth, 2020; Maxwell, 2013).

To validate the research, I took multiple steps (see table 1). I remained vigilant of potential researcher bias through reflection and bracketing techniques. Epoché and bracketing were employed to prevent these biases from devaluing conclusions. The inclusion of knowledgeable interviewees with diverse perspectives on the phenomenon, mitigated and limited bias. These participants served as cases that offered retrospective sense-making and theory-building opportunities.

Reactivity, "the researcher's effect on the setting or the people being studied,"[12] is another common threat to validity. The key to controlling validity threats in a qualitative inquiry is to understand their potential influence, not to eliminate them entirely. Multiple methodologies, including interviews, a focus group, observation notes, and descriptive statistical data from archival documents, to triangulate data and mitigate these validity threats. Additionally, participants reviewed transcripts for accuracy, ensuring their voices and stories were genuinely represented. Lastly, to address internal generalizability, purposeful sampling included Black women superintendents from diverse school settings, and mixed data sources were utilized to strengthen insights.

Theory-building case studies offer a rigorous yet flexible methodology for illuminating under-researched experiences. By utilizing Eisenhardt's process and a multifaceted approach to data collection, analysis, and interpretation, researchers can move beyond merely describing phenomena to generating new theories grounded in the lived realities of those often marginalized in traditional research. This methodology holds immense promise for expanding our understanding of complex social issues and informing more equitable and inclusive practices in research and policy development across various fields, including educational leadership.

Notes

1 Hurston, Z. N. (1942). *Dust tracks on a road* (p. 91). Arno.

2 Eisenhardt, K. M., & Graebner, M. E. (2007). Theory building from cases: Opportunities and challenges. *Academy of Management Journal*, 50(1), 25–32, 30.

3 Eisenhardt, 1989.

4 I. Introduction/Background

Brief introduction of study/obtain informed consent.
When did you first become a superintendent? How long were you a superintendent?
Of which race/ethnicity and gender do you self-identify?

II. Accessibility to the Superintendency

Why did you want to become a superintendent?
Do you believe the superintendent pipeline is exclusive?
That Black women are underrepresented in the field?
Why might that be?
Describe your career trajectory leading to the position of Superintendent.
How were you recruited for the superintendency role?
Were there obstacles that limited access or attainment?
Have you faced any discrimination, bias, or gaslighting in the job search/hiring process? Please explain.
Did you have a sponsor that advocated for your appointment/hiring? Please explain.
Did your university connect, sponsor or support your trajectory? Please explain.
Did a search firm consultant connect, support, and/or advocate for your trajectory to the superintendency? Please explain.
Describe the search, interview, and hiring process for the superintendency. Do you feel the hiring process was fair?

III. Barriers/Challenges faced in the trajectory to and in the role of the Superintendency

What barriers did you face in your trajectory to the superintendency (headship)?

Were there barriers unique to being a woman?
Were there barriers unique to being Black?
Did you feel the barriers you experienced were different from Black men?
Different from White women?
Describe the challenges you faced as a Black woman superintendent moving into a role traditionally and historically held by White males?
Did you experience any social, cultural, or familial factors that influenced your decision to become a superintendent?
How did you overcome these barriers and challenges?
Describe your retention and tenure in the superintendency role. Why do you stay in the role?
Explain the influence or impact of the Board of Trustees, if any
What factors were barriers to retention?
What are some factors that support your trajectory to the superintendency?
What factors help you stay in the role/position?

IV. Experiences in the Superintendency

What type of K–12 school do you serve as superintendent?
What type of student body do you serve?
What is your relationship like with the Board?
teachers/leaders
parents/students
Do you feel supported by your Board? Explain why or why not 20. How have your experiences influenced your leadership style/practice?
What type of leader are you?
How would you describe your strengths and weaknesses as a leader?
What are the highlights of your superintendency thus far (i.e., policies put in place etc.)
If you could write a prelude to your memoirs/story of your life as a superintendent, what would it say?
Why did you become a superintendent/head? Do you feel you have achieved or accomplished what you set out to do?
What did it feel like when you initially entered (or the first few years) the superintendency? What changed by your 5th year and/or 2nd superintendency? Explain the major differences, if any, from the initial start of your superintendency to the retirement year of your superintendency.

V. Call for Change: Suggestions/Actions to Improve Diversity, Equity, and Inclusivity in the Superintendency

What are the benefits of Black women (WOC) serving in the superintendency role?
What advice would you offer other Black women aspiring to be a superintendent?
What do you think needs to be changed to make the superintendent pipeline more diverse, equitable, and inclusive?
What practices and changes do they believe can help "break the glass ceiling" to increase
Black women (WOC) into the superintendent pool?

VI. Concluding Comment and Questions

31. Is there anything else regarding race, gender, and your experience in the superintendency role that you would like to share?

Thank you for participating in this study.

5 The purpose of this focus group is to capture your perception of the impact race and gender has on the acquisition and retention of the superintendent. There is no right or wrong response. Your voice and experience are valued. Please feel comfortable expressing your thoughts and saying what you think and feel. The zoom conversation will be recorded and transcribed. Inquiry for Focus Group will help investigate the following research questions:

RQ1. What challenges and supports have Black women superintendents and heads encountered in taking on their roles and leading their schools?

RQ2. From the perspective of these women, how can the superintendent/headship pipeline be more inclusive for Black women?

Confidential Practices

In agreeing to participate in this study/inquiry, confidentiality is expected and up to all participants. We may discuss sensitive issues and familiar colleagues; it is important that all participants agree to and adhere to the confidential agreement discussed/signed.

I. Introduction

Explain study inquiry, review consent, and confidentiality expectations

Introduce myself as the moderator and share my connection and interest to the study

II. Demographic Questions

Have all focus group panelists introduce them, providing demographics:

What region are they from? And served as superintendent?

How many years have they been a superintendent

Background heritage/race/ethnicity/gender

Highest level of education?

What administrative/leadership roles did you serve in prior to becoming a superintendent?

Why did you become a superintendent/HOS? What was your leadership style?

III. Perception and Experiences

What do you think made your resume and interview successful?

Who controls succession, access, and appointment to the superintendency?

What barriers have you witnessed in your path to superintendency?

What barriers/challenges have you experienced in the superintendency role?

Do Black women create their own barriers?

Do you think recruiters and job postings encourage Black women superintendents?

Over 30 years ago, Kimberlé Crenshaw (a law professor at Columbia and UCLA) coined the term *intersectionality*. Intersectionality refers to the intertwined forms of inequalities that often operate simultaneously and even exacerbate each other. *Do you think intersecting identities of race* and *gender are contributing factors for the underrepresentation of WOC in the superintendency?*

In 2000, U.S. Census named the K–12 school superintendency as the most White male-dominated executive leadership position. Do you agree? Explain why or why not.
Do you think the superintendent pipeline is inclusive of all races and gender so long as you have the right qualifications?
Why do you think Black women superintendents (HOS) are so underrepresented in the pipeline compared to White women or Black male superintendent counterparts?
As a superintendent (HOS) have you experienced any biases, microaggressions, gaslighting, or discrimination? If so, can you tell us about that experience?
How did it make you feel?
How did you deal with, handle, and overcome it?

IV. Call to Action

How do you mentor other Black women or WOC for the superintendency?
How can the search and hiring processes be changed to be more inclusive? What needs to change?
What role should universities play? Boards? search firms? And what role do sitting superintendents play in making the superintendent pipeline more diverse and inclusive?
What practices do you believe can help "break the glass ceiling" to increase more Black women in the superintendent pool?
Is there anything else you'd like to share or ask the other panelist?
Thank you for participating in this study.

6 I recorded the Zoom focus group interview in video and audio so I could go back and review context, physical expressions, voice tone, and behavior.

7 Document analysis is a qualitative method for reviewing and analyzing electronic and printed sources.

8 Eisenhardt, K. M. (1989). Building theory from case study research. *Academy of Management Review, 14*(4), 532–550, 538.

9 Dooley asserted that the usage of different types of data, different participants as cases, and an additional investigator:

> Keeps the researcher from being blinded by vivid but potentially misleading impressions presented in the form of qualitative data. At the same time, qualitative data can be important in building an understanding of the theory underlying the relationships revealed in quantitative data (p. 345).

Dooley, L. M. (2002). Case study research and theory building. *Advances in Developing Human Resources, 4*(3), 335–354.

10 Miles, M. B., Huberman, M. A., & Saldaña, J. (2020). *Qualitative data analysis: A methods sourcebook* (4th ed.). Sage.

11 Eisenhardt & Graebner, 2007, p. 29, italics in the original.

12 Maxwell, J. A. (2013). *Qualitative research design: An interactive approach* (3rd ed., p. 124). Sage.

· 4 ·

HERSTORIES: SIX BLACK WOMEN SUPERINTENDENTS-HEADS

There is no greater agony than bearing an untold story inside you.

—Maya Angelou[1]

Literature Review on Black Women Superintendents

Previous research paints a consistent picture of Black women superintendents: highly qualified and experienced leaders. They typically possess strong educational and experiential backgrounds. All held master's degrees, and most had doctorates. Their career trajectories typically began as classroom teachers, followed by a traditional pathway through principalships. Over half served as assistant or deputy superintendents prior to their superintendency and some held state department administrative positions.

Beyond their formal qualifications, studies also highlighted that these women were affiliated with community and professional organizations. Almost all were members of organizations such as the the Association for Supervision and Curriculum Development, the AASA, Phi Delta Kappa, and/or the National Alliance of Black School Educators. Their involvement often extends to community, local, or state organizations that influenced school policy such as the Rotary, Chamber of Commerce, YMCA, Kiwanis, hospitals, libraries, and other youth-serving institutions. Many also held leadership titles on their sorority and church governing boards.

Despite their impressive credentials and community engagement, Black women remain disproportionately underrepresented in the superintendency. This raises a critical question: why does this disparity persist?

Data Disparities

A major issue is the lack of diversity among those who control access to the superintendency pipeline. The gatekeepers of superintendent appointments, primarily White male search firm consultants and school boards, often prioritize candidates who mirror their own demographics and experiences. This entrenched power dynamic creates little incentive to dismantle a system they benefit from.

Using a critical race theory lens, Jackson and Shakeshaft explained how "interest convergence"[2] and the "ordinariness of racism"[3] hinder Blacks from accessing the superintendency. Underrepresented candidates are often pigeonholed into serving minority school districts, and the multilayered hiring process creates increased opportunities for bias at each stage.

Alston identified the following five barriers Black women encounter in their trajectory to the superintendency:

1. Lack of support systems or sponsorship (i.e., "old boy network");
2. Lack of role models;
3. Unawareness of political maneuvers;
4. Societal stereotypes regarding Black women's competencies;
5. Lack of structured programs for identifying aspiring Black superintendents.[4]

Despite the progress made by those who successfully attain the superintendency, Alston warned with great urgency that the number of Black women in these roles is declining. This is due in part to the persistent discrimination, often subtle and disguised, that continues throughout their tenure in the role. "Unlike overt acts of bigotry that are punishable by law, subtle bias wends through workplaces like an odorless vapor that when left unchecked, stirs up feelings in Black women that range from frustration to apathy to anger."[5]

Black women are grossly underrepresented in the superintendency. One challenge in addressing this issue is the lack of comprehensive data on the number of female superintendents, particularly women of color.[6] Even in an age of advanced data collection, there are no consistent official reports on the number of Black women superintendents in the United States. Considering the importance of such information in understanding educational leadership, this absence is concerning.

A 2000 NYSCOSS study found that while women made up 40% of the newly hired superintendents in New York State, only 1.5% were people of color.[7] Jackson and Shakeshaft[8] further examined the demographics of superintendents and revealed significant disparities in the hiring process in Long Island's Nassau and Suffolk counties. Of the 550 applicants for 12 vacancies:

- 70.9% of White male applicants were interviewed.
- 22.7% of White female applicants were interviewed.
- 4.4% of Black male applicants were interviewed.
- 1.2% of Black female applicants were interviewed.

This data highlights a clear pattern of preferential hiring based on gender and race, favoring White males. Nationally, the data echo these trends. In 1993, only 20 out 1,980 female superintendents were Black.[9] By the early 2000s, this number had barely increased, with 91.6% of female superintendents being White and only 5.1% Black.[10]

Ethnocentric ways of knowing and leading schools are not isolated to any particular region of the United States or the world. For example, Fitzgerald's[11] research on indigenous women in education leadership highlighted the double challenge women in New Zealand, Australia, and Canada faced walking in the overlap of the two worlds of gender and ethnicity. Because schools locally and globally are designed to serve the interests of the dominant group, research, policies, and practices tend to overlook or even disadvantage marginalized individuals. This, Fitzgerald asserted, is a reflection of the direct issue of power, authority, and differences across and between the lines of ethnicity and gender.

Data on women in the superintendency are often based on limited surveys and are nonexistent for women of color. Moreover, in an age marked by technological innovation and enumeration of data, it was extraordinarily striking to learn there are no ongoing official data reports on the number of Black women superintendents in the United States, likewise abroad. Considering the importance of such information in educational leadership literature, this does not seem unintentional.

Relationships have been identified as a key component to attaining and retaining superintendencies. In fact, many studies[12] revealed that Black women and Latina superintendents experienced loneliness associated with the superintendent job.

Brown[13] asserted that the struggles Black women face in attaining superintendency are directly related to systemic challenges in U.S. democracy that require women of color to mask their true identities to be what White society would have them be. In her study of Latina superintendents, Méndez-Morse[14] identified "redefinition" as a major challenge—a process where women of color grapple with shifting self-perception and identities amidst the isolation and scrutiny of the role. As the study noted, "it gets very lonely, very fast, at the top,"[15] findings repeatedly expressed the importance of having a support system to combat the isolation. Although the participants felt they were the same person prior to attaining the top job, they recognized that others saw them "through a different lens."[16] Méndez-Morse concluded that the superintendency (the metamorphosis phrase) was a "striking alteration" in how others viewed these leaders.[17]

Similarly, Ortiz[18] concluded that this isolation is one of the major factors contributing to the underrepresentation of women of color in the superintendency. Coping mechanisms for this isolation and the pressure to "mask" one's identity are not always healthy. Avoidance, denial, disconnect, and resignation were noted as maladaptive strategies for gendered racism.[19] As Brown illustrated, participants shared that they did not complain when pervasive or subtle acts of bias or microaggressions were perpetrated against them because they feared looking "weak and whiny"[20] and being accused of playing the "race card."[21]

Ortiz revealed that lack of sponsored and executive appointments by personal contact affected mobility. Successful Hispanic superintendents in her study developed the connections and understood the interdependence between symbolic and professional expectations. Ortiz emphasized the importance of establishing extensive networks and relationships. The most successful participants had support sponsors. Notably, those with White male sponsors also had favorable contracts.

The AASA and the National School Boards Association identified the tenure of exemplary superintendents as 8.5 years, contrasted with the national figure of 6.2 years. Sponsors included current and former superintendents, board members, and even university professors. Ortiz found that sponsorships correlated with longer tenure.

Ortiz introduced the concept of "social capital" as a crucial resource that is susceptible to reciprocity "through structures of personal relationships and strong networks."[22] This resource facilitated cooperation, trust, and collective action, which served as an additional resource for women of color superintendents. According to Ortiz, participants' ascension to the superintendency resembled a kinship structure embedded in the relationships they had with the school district community. More specifically to Latina superintendents, the community's culture, land, and language were exclusive and made these towns uninviting to outsiders. This created opportunities for Latina women superintendents.

Rodriguez[23] corroborated Ortiz's findings, reporting that social capital, including professional networks, family, and community members were instrumental in initiating superintendency searches and search consultants connections.

Across these studies, the impact of Black women superintendents' relationship with the board was evident. Closely related to the scarcity in the field, Alston[24] asserted that aspiring Black women superintendent often have a challenging time finding other Black women mentors and sponsors. This, Alston shared, is coupled with a societal lack of acceptance for cultural diversity and a preference for White males in the profession.

Memberships in associations, churches, committees, and sororities also proved helpful. Brown[25] found that building trust and establishing connections with sponsors, mentors, board trustees, church community members, and even the media helped to improve retention in the role. Burton et al.[26] similarly found engaging with professional networks, faith-based groups, and other social relations groupings served as affirming and adaptive ways Black women leaders overcame gendered racism-related barriers.

Finally, I want to note here that researchers have found that women of color's trajectory to the superintendency appeared to influence how they led their schools. Black women, Alston[27] asserted, turn their adversities into inspiration that often makes them tempered radicals and servant leaders. She described Black women superintendents as tempered radicals who possess tenacity, who are committed to their institution, and are often at odds with White supremacy culture. Their leadership styles are collaborative, and they are activists in their roles. Jean-Marie et al. found that Black women's "transcendence of racial and gender stereotypes" became the incentive for developing leadership styles that were collaborative and inclusive.[28] Black women superintendents are often servant leaders who are collaborative, inclusive, and courageously willing to rock the boat.

The existing literature highlights the challenges and complexities faced by Black women in educational leadership, particularly in their pursuit and experience in the superintendency. It also underscores the importance of relationships, social capital, and mentorship in navigating these challenges. The following sections will delve deeper into the experiences of six Black women superintendents, providing nuanced insights into their individual journeys and the systemic barriers they encounter.

A Theory-Based Sampling

Given the limited number of Black women superintendents, I employed a purposeful, theory-based sampling strategy to recruit sitting women superintendents who self-identified as Black or African American. This approach reduced extraneous variables and aligned with the criteria of intersectionality theory. I recruited participants from various professional associations, including LinkedIn, the AASA, the NAIS, and local New York State associations. Recruitment letters[29] were sent to eligible participants and associations.

The resulting participant pool represented a cross-section of superintendents, with tenures ranging from their first year to those with over a decade of experience. This purposeful sampling strategy targeted participants who aligned with the criteria and theoretical constructs of intersectionality and the phenomenon being studied, specifically, K–12 superintendency. Participants were recruited with the aid of professional networks. In this study, choosing participants who could contribute to theory development was particularly important, as this inquiry aimed to refine or even generate new theory.

To maximize variation, I employed a popular approach in which researchers intentionally diversify their sample. Here, participants fitting the demographic criteria were selected from a variety of settings. This included variations in type of school institution, district communities, demographics, and level of expertise/tenure.

Nine potential participants were indentified through professional associations and LinkedIn. Initial contact with independent school heads was facilitated through the NAIS vice president for studies, insights, and research, who granted permission to proceed after learning about the study's purpose and my background.[30] Two Black women heads agreed to participate, and were contacted.

For sitting public school Black women superintendents, I sent emails to six qualifying candidates. After several unanswered attempts, I contacted the superintendents' assistants. Five agreed and signed the informed consent. Of these, four participated in either one-on-one interviews or focus group.

Ultimately, six Black women superintendents (including heads of schools) from two regions within New York State all signed consent forms[31] agreeing to participate in the study. Four engaged in one-on-one interviews, whereas two participated exclusively in the focus group. Given the small population sample and the need to protect participants from identification and harm, pseudonyms based on perfume names were assigned, and identifiable demographic data excluded.

Dr. Dior, one of the participants, powerfully asserted:

> This is my voice. I'm so excited about being able to use my voice and use my voice in the way, in stages. I'm 73 and in stages, you get to the point where you say, "Wait a minute, uh-huh, who's the one that's going to stand up and tell you what you should have known years ago?" That's where I am right now, I am almost repenting for the time that I couldn't or didn't, not couldn't, but didn't, and so you have to know who's the voice.

HerStory: Giving Voice to the Hybrid Identity

While existing literature is scarce, it still clearly reveals that the voices of Black women heads and superintendents have been largely unheard or overshadowed by their counterparts. This research aims to capture the untold stories of these women serving in New York State. Following Revere's framework, subthemes emerged around family ties, pathways to leadership, and the motivations and impact of their leadership, providing insight into the participants' identities, and their experiences.

The overarching theme of, "HerStory" emerged from the individual interviews and focus group discussion. Each participant's unique story and profile contribute to a collective narrative that illuminates the rich and varied experiences of Black women in leadership positions.

To protect participant confidentiality while still providing a glimpse into their backgrounds, Table 2 presents a summary of their profiles, including pseudonyms, race/ethnicity, parental status, highest degree earned, school

Table 2 *Participant Profiles*

Participant Pseudonym	Race/Ethnicity	Children	Highest Degree	School Type	Years in Education	Years in Superintendent-Head Role
Ms. Chanel	Black woman (Caribbean roots)	Two young children	Master's degree	Independent (K-8)	16	2
Dr. Le Labo	Black woman (Caribbean roots)	Adult child and grandchild	Doctorate	Public (K-12)	Over 40	17
Dr. Ambrosia	Black woman	Six children	Doctorate	Public (K-12)	28	2
Dr. Valentino	Black woman	Two children	Doctorate	Independent (PreK-12)	Over 30	4
Dr. Fenty	Black woman (Caribbean roots)	Three adult children	Doctorate	Public (K-6)	Over 30	1.5
Dr. Dior	Black woman	None mentioned	Doctorate	Public (K-12)	50	14

type, years in education, and years in their current superintendent/head of school role.

Using intersectionality as a framework for this theory-building case study and its findings, "places the experiences of Black women at the center of the analysis in producing new knowledge about intersecting forms of oppression that impact educational opportunities, economic freedom, and political enfranchisement."[32] Essentially, intersectionality serves as a discourse for producing new knowledge about intersecting forms of oppression that impact educational opportunities and leadership trajectories.

HerStory #1: Dr. Le Labo

Dr. Le Labo, a seasoned educator with over 40 years of experience, was interviewed during her 17th year as superintendent of a racially diverse K–12 suburban school district. This marked her third superintendency, with prior leadership roles in high-performing districts characterized as majority White populations and a high socioeconomic demographics.

Born and raised in Jamaica, West Indies, Dr. Le Labo's upbringing instilled a deep appreciation for education. She shared, "education was always going to be the place where I was going to succeed." Recalling poverty as the first barrier in her life, she saw a good education was a means to escape poverty and achieve success. Reminiscing, she sang a childhood mantra,

> "Labor for learning before you grow old. For learning is better than silver or gold. Silver and gold will vanish away but a good education will never decay."

Raised by her aunt, a single guardian and teacher, Dr. Le Labo began her academic journey at the tender age of three, accompaning her aunt to work as there was no one to watch her. "Nobody told me that a 3-year-old couldn't learn, so I learned." Dr. Le labo attended an all-girls school where she excelled in mathematics, physics, and similar fields. She pursued higher education in the states, a university in New York, where she was the only woman of color.

Following graduate school, Dr. Le Labo embarked on a teaching career in independent and public schools in New York State. Her path to the CEO superintendency role was a traditional one, ascending through the ranks as a teacher, chair, instructional supervisor, assistant principal, director, assistant superintendent, and then superintendent.

Interestingly, the superintendency, was not an initial aspiration. In fact, Dr. Le Labo recalled she expected to lose her job when she was offered her first instructional leadership role. Budget cuts and constraints resulted in the elimination of the chair role, which was a percentage of her teaching load. At best, she hoped not to lose her job altogether but to pick up additional teaching assignments so she could be full-time. Dr. Le Labo was 26 years old at this time, and had already earned her doctorate in science. Shocked that Dr. Le Labo had already earned her doctorate, her superintendent denied her request to teach additional classes and offered her an instructional supervisory role. Dr. Le Labo responded with appreciation but shared, "Yeah, that sounds great, but… I don't have my administrative license." Moreover, she did not have any education credits. Her superintendent told her to go get them, and that is just what she did. While teaching at the university and in the school district, Dr. Le Labo took education credits and earned her administrative leadership license by the summer of that year.

A recipient of NAACP and other awards, Dr. Le Labo is recognized for her contributions to detracking students, data-driven school improvement, and promoting equity and access in student learning. She has also actively participated in many professional associations, focusing her efforts on eradicating racism and advancing social justice.

A "happily" divorced parent and grandparent, Dr. Le labo maintains strong ties to her family and Jamaican roots. Her passion, confidence, and strong will resonated throughout the interview. When questioned about her longevity as a superintendent and her superpowers, Dr. Le Labo attributed her success to her limitless personality, echoing Eleanor Roosevelt's sentiment of not allowing others to set limits for you. She said, "I think my personality has no limits… Sort of like Eleanor Roosevelt always said, 'You can't insult me unless I gave you permission to do that.' You can't set a limit for me unless I give you permission to do that."

HerStory #2: Ms. Chanel

Ms. Chanel, a married mother with two young children, was serving her second year as the head of an affluent New York State K–8 independent school, where she previously held another role. The school community is racially diverse and maintains strong but separate ties with a nearby religious institution, "where there has been a very long and well-established relationship to social justice... [eagerly] bringing that into everything that we do."

Born and partially raised in New York, Ms. Chanel proudly identifies as a "Strong Island" native, though her family relocated to Tennessee during her childhood; an experience she never fully embraced. Asserting, "I found my way back up here as fast as I could." Ms. Chanel eagerly returned to New York and maintains family ties in the Caribbean. When describing her background, Ms. Chanel shared the following:

> I am Black American, regular Black, mostly. I go back to Barbados on my father's side with the great-grandparent front, but not a direct cultural engagement in my family growing up, so I just tell folks I am good and regular Black and happy for it.

Ms. Chanel self-describes as a successful product of public schools, where here own children are also enrolled. When asked how she manages motherhood and her career, Ms. Chanel smiled, credited her supportive husband saying, "I have a partner at home, and he's incredible in all the ways as a parent and as a partner."

Ms. Chanel's career path differed from other participants in this study. Her background in school leadership extends beyond an instructional track. Rather it was grounded in development, communication, fundraising, community engagement and diversity, equity, and inclusion work. Before becoming a teacher, Ms. Chanel worked for renowned national museums, state organizations, and associations. Additionally, she served as a school board trustee and co-founded a leadership institute for aspiring leaders. She said, "I've started a number of leadership programs for folks, generally focused on independent schools, recognizing that they are different from the needs and expectations, and responsibilities that come with public school settings."

Becoming head of school was never Ms. Chanel's intention. She did not participate in a leadership or aspiring leader programs. She believed the role was attainable and the work important, but she did not actively seek it out. In fact, she recalled making recommendations for other candidates. This, her current role, was a school she loved and felt deeply connected to. So when the opportunity arose to suggest potential candidates for head of school, she eagerly did, just not her own. Then one day, the search consultant at the placement firm surprised her, saying, "We keep hearing your name."

Ms. Chanel laughed as she recounted, "And I thought, 'Well, that's silly, but I do want to start interviewing, so let me just see what happens.' And this is what happened."

Ms. Chanel described herself as a "warm demander" someone who values relationships while holding herself and others accountable. She asserted, I would define a warm demander... [as] somebody who values a relationship between myself and other people. And through that relationship making it very clear that I care about that person, but also that I have high expectations for them that I know they can reach; that are not beyond their capability; and that I will help them reach. But also, that they're going to do that thing. It is not up for discussion.

Building on this philosophy, Ms. Chanel explained that there is a responsibility, inherited value and accountability inherent in leadership, particularly for Black women:

> In this country, our tolerance for pain is so much higher in a way that schools benefit from. It's terrible for us, but schools certainly benefit from it because there's just the ability to deal with it. And the understanding that the only way out is through and not melting down on a regular basis or lashing out at folks on a regular basis, because it's not going to solve anything, it hasn't for us for hundreds of years.

Despite being the youngest head-superintendent in the study, Ms. Chanel embodied a spirit of possibility, as her community would described it. This spirit has brought out the best in both her and the community she serves.

HerStory #3: Dr. Valentino

Dr. Valentino was in the 4th year of her first tenure as head of school at an independent school serving pre-K–12 students. The school is geographically, racially, and socioeconomically diverse. Dr. Valentino noted, "A number of families are on aid, but many, many families are not. And in one way, it's challenging to really know... People don't have to supply that information unless they are looking to receive aid."

Born and raised in Chicago, Dr. Valentino shared that her passion for learning and education began at an early age, sparked and inspired by her teachers. Attending a public, Catholic, single-gender school that became co-ed the year she started, inclusive education shaped her interest in teaching, her choice of schools, and her scholarly pursuits. This environment also impacted her personal life.

Dr. Valentino met her husband at university, where they both studied, and have two children. She also serves on the board of trustees of that university.

Dr. Valentino credits her mother, who passed away a few years ago, as a significant influence on who she is and how she leads:

> My mom passed away a few years ago; she really was the beacon in my life. This amazing person with people and that too I guess I would say in terms of the headship. I think being a person who enjoys people and who even when people are being confronted with stress, that sense of this is again about teaching and learning. I think that really helps you out. She was a great teacher and a great grandma.

At university, Dr. Valentino's interest in history deepened, particularly, the history of marginalized people and the Black woman's experience. With the encouragement of the educators in her life, Dr. Valentino discovered her voice and love for academia. This, along with her understanding the importance of scholarship, influenced her decision to go back to school to pursue her PhD. Her dissertation focused on New York City public schools. Research, justice, and excellence continued to motivate her passion. So, despite her love for academia, she was drawn back to students and resumed a career teaching in independent schools.

Dr. Valentino did set out to become a head of school. Her career path included roles as a teacher and advisor. She worked in admissions, became the high-school principal and assistant head of school. In addition to these roles, she also actively engaged in diversity, equity, and inclusivity work, all of which she felt helped to prepare her for the headship. Dr. Valentino shared:

> I did a lot of things that heads of school do, making asks for philanthropic contributions to the school, really navigating dicey public relations issues, dealing with discipline, dealing with faculty support.

These experiences led her mentors to encourage her. Dr. Valentino explained:

> So, I ended up doing so many things that were similar to being head of school that at one point I was being encouraged by my mentors to just go ahead and put my hat in that ring, and it started to make increasingly more sense to me to do so.

Dr. Valentino is well-known for her interpersonal skills, problem-solving abilities, and her capacity to see the big picture from multiple perspectives. Her community described her as courageous and adept at navigating difficult situations and conversations. Despite the challenges posed by the racial reckoning and the pandemic, Dr. Valentino remains proud of her community and leadership approach. She asserted:

> I'm really proud of the way that I have tried to help my school community in the face of these fairly turbulent times, how I have sought a cohesion in the community that is an honest cohesion. So not like rose-tinted glasses, but rather a deep communication and commitment.

HerStory #4 Dr. Ambrosia

Similar to Ms. Chanel, Dr. Ambrosia was serving the second year of her first superintendency. She led a suburban K–12 school district and had worked in education for 28 years. Her school district was racially and socioeconomically diverse. A large majority of students were from the Americas, primarily El Salvador, Honduras, and Belize, with a small Asian population, students of African descent, and a strong Caribbean population, both English and Creole speaking. Dr. Ambrosia explained that Black women were frequently invited to lead in districts "where the house is on fire" and on a variety of complex issues. However, she proudly proclaimed, "My district is not on fire at all... We do have some issues around poverty but we are a good district."

Dr. Ambrosia was no stranger to poverty herself. She grew up in a section of New York that had its share of inequities, economically and educationally. She recalled a profound moment in her middle years. Having had an opportunity to be an exchange student in Panamá, it left an impression on her:

> I was in middle school, an exchange student in Panama... And Panama, as you know, is a very racially diverse Latin American country... This was the early '80s... there was a mayor, an alcalde, of Panama City... a brown-skinned man, darker than me, with an afro. And I just remember, I'll never forget, just remembering a mayor could have an afro? A mayor can be Black?... I just assumed that mayors are White people. Very specifically, mayors are White men.

A person who had great influence on Dr. Ambrosia was her maternal grandmother. She was a NYPD officer and moved up the ranks to later become a lieutenant correction officer, a nontraditional role for women at the time. She shared:

> My grandmother carried a gun that made me think like, "Damn, women can do whatever they want to do. My grandma's a badass. She carries a gun in the supermarket."

> And there was a lot of respect she had for the job. And a lot of respect people have for her.

Dr. Ambrosia shared that as a teenage mother she was supported and built a resiliency that helps her to lead today. Dr. Ambrosia is happily married and attributed much of her success to her husband and family. She is the proud mother of six children. She stated, "If I can start college with a 5-month-old, and I'm still breastfeeding, and graduate with all my peers, who start at the same time, I could do near anything."

These experiences, among others, fueled Dr. Ambrosia's passion and commitment to helping young people facing challenges. She strives to ensure all students have access to a high-quality education that empowers them and fully prepares them for college, careers, and life. Dr. Ambrosia acknowledged:

> So, like Snoop Dogg says, shout out to me. I didn't let anybody write me off. But more importantly, there were so many people who just poured into me and let me know, at a very pivotal moment in my development, that despite being a young mother, I could really accomplish anything I wanted.

Dr. Ambrosia is a highly qualified and experienced educator with a strong desire to lead. She holds a Ph.D. and has served in various leadership roles, including founding principal, executive director, assistant superintendent, and adjunct lecturer who taught education leadership to aspiring administrators. Dr. Ambrosia shared, "I wasn't recruited. I applied." No one recruited her for the superintendency, but she knew she wanted to do this job: "I believe that our children deserve strong, competent leaders who are reflective of their community. And I felt like I had the vision and the will to do it."

Dr. Ambrosia's superpowers are described as being a strong listener and big-picture thinker who can adapt. She is goal oriented and collaborative. Dr. Ambrosia reflected and shared, "even though I can be very, very stubborn, I really do listen... marinate on it and shift if need be."

HerStory #5: Dr. Fenty

Dr. Fenty, a participant in the focus group panel, brings a background in marketing and special education, to her first year as superintendent of a K–6 suburban school district in New York State. Like Ms. Chanel, she was a former employee of that school. Prior to her superintendent appointment, Dr. Fenty served as an interim superintendent in another New York State school district. She has also served as an administrator in other states besides New York, including Georgia, North Carolina, and Florida.

The proud mother of three adult children and two grandchildren, Dr. Fenty has lived in New York for over 45 years. She holds a doctorate in education and identified as a Black American woman with Cuban and Jamaican roots. This intersectionality, she asserted, has led to some "othering" because of her multiple identities:

> I'm a woman, and I'm Cuban and Jamaican, and I was raised in both cultures, and I appreciated Chanel's comment about being a Black American, I think it's a very different experience. Actually, I learned that from [people in the previous school district]... I was like, so I'm Black... Then, once everyone found out that I was Caribbean, the jokes, 14 jobs, and then, "Oh, wait a minute, you're Spanish." ... There was some othering, and I was really shocked about it. I had to call my mother; I was like, "So, I'm not Black? I'm so confused. What am I?"

This experience led Dr. Fenty to recognize "and develop a deeper appreciation for the Black experience" because it is as diverse as its people. She learned and recognized that the African American and Caribbean American journeys in America were not always the same, and she is committed to understanding these nuances to better support her community.

Committed to ensuring children do not feel stigmatized for their differences, Dr. Fenty champions equity and inclusion. She connected to the community and chose to lead in a place where she could develop "equitable, inclusive, and sustainable solutions for the greater good of humanity."

In the focus group panel, Dr. Fenty commented on how important it is for young women to have role models in leadership positions who celebrate the authenticity and beauty of Black women:

> It's much bigger than [that]... It is freedom that you're able to know [that hair can be in its natural form] that's helping the young children to realize that, unlike all of us who, remember, we were... getting our hair pressed, getting burnt ears and third-degree burns, that they don't have to go through this. I've seen little children who, parents have put relaxers in their hair years ago and their scalp was now totally damaged, because there was this need to look like someone who has power, who has privilege, and yet, we have the power... in our hair.

Dr. Fenty explained that this is why she and other women in the study often chose to wear their hair in its natural curls. A Black woman's crown—her hair—is historically and socially significant, representing her glory, privilege, and power.

HerStory #6: Dr. Dior

Dr. Dior, a participant in the focus group panel, was known by many as a reformist and fixer. With over 50 years of experience in education, she has transformed struggling districts in Maryland, Philadelphia, and New York into successful learning environments. Dr. Dior had served as superintendent in Philadelphia and two New York public school districts, one of which she was invited back to lead almost a decade later. At the time of the panel, Dr. Dior was the superintendent of a large, diverse suburban New York State public school with a challenging history. The school district was almost entirely composed of students of color, mainly Blacks and Latinx with more than 45% economically disadvantaged.

Like Dr. Valentino, Dr. Dior was born and raised in Chicago, Illinois. She was one of five children. From a very early age, Dr. Dior's father instilled in her and her siblings the importance of education, telling them, telling them, "You have to go to college, and your mother and I have no money, so you have to get a scholarship." So, from kindergarten, she and her siblings all knew they were going to college on a scholarship, which is what she did. Earning the Martin Luther King, Jr. scholarship, Dr. Dior went to a university about three hours away. There, she was one of only 50 African Americans among 33,000 students. Dr. Dior smiled and asserted, "So, I left the university... with three As: a degree, a man, and membership in the Alpha Kappa Alpha sorority. That man I met became my husband."

Even after all these years, Dr. Dior still blushed when she speaks of her husband, "I'm still in love," and told the panel group about when they first met:

> I met my husband on the first day of college. I was hungry... I went to the student union to get something to eat with my roommate. My husband and his roommate, they were looking for food, as well, only the female food, so it was not love at first sight, but a week after graduation, we got married. He is from Maryland... I'm in love, I'm going to follow my heart and move to Maryland, such a fairytale story... my husband... he was such a supporter.

So, she followed her heart and passion to Maryland, where her career as an educator began.

Dr. Dior holds doctorate degree and has spent 36 years in Maryland public schools. She said:

> I am the proud owner of a doctorate in educational leadership and I have served in every role known to man leading up to the superintendency... teacher, teacher of the

> year, curriculum specialist, director of professional development, assistant superintendent, and superintendent, so I am excited about my walk and my role. The one thing that's significant about me is that I am an ordained licensed minister, and my faith is my work and my work is my faith.

Dr. Dior served in various positions, eventually retiring as an assistant superintendent to pursue her first superintendency in Philadelphia. She explained:

> Women, African American women specifically… [you learn] that you will have to relocate, and so I drove an hour over the Maryland line to Pennsylvania and that was my first superintendency, 1,200 students. There were 500 districts in Pennsylvania. It was District Number 498 from the bottom. We did that work there, and then I was actually recruited to go to another district in Pennsylvania, and they were 497 from the bottom. So, both of those districts were resurrected, and it was clear to me that I was called to be a superintendent of districts that were not number 1 yet.

When Dr. Dior was interviewing for another superintendent position in California, all of her references gave her negative reviews because they didn't want her to leave. However, she pursued the opportunity anyway. At the end of the interview for that California job, the headhunter said, "This is not good for you. You need to be in New York." And New York is where she ended up. After successfully leading and "fixing" that district, Dr. Dior moved on to another district within the state for five years. Then, the board of her original district invited her back, saying, "Come home." So she returned to the district where it all began in New York, where she is still serving, a little more than a decade later. Dr. Dior reflected, "This is where I belong."

In reflecting on these school leaders' herstories, it's clear that intersectionality is a crucial framework for understanding their experiences. Their accounts reveal how their intersecting identities as Black women, educators, and leaders have shaped their journeys, views, and outcomes. These profiles highlight the communities the participants served, their family backgrounds, and their unique paths in the superintendent/head role. The profiles reveal the common social identities shared by all participants: being Black, being a woman, and being a superintendent/head. The totality of these intersecting social identities, Black (race), women (gender), and superintendents/heads (role)—creates a distinct, hybrid identity that transcends the individual social constructs. Thus, the convergence of race, gender, and professional role creates a unique experience for Black women in educational leadership that cannot be fully understood by examining these identities in isolation. This chapter has laid the groundwork for understanding the unique context and experiences of Black women in educational leadership, setting the stage for a deeper exploration of their individual stories and the insights they offer into the complexities of intersectionality in this field. As you read through the other chapters in this book, you will gain a deeper understanding of how this hybrid, intersecting identity manifests itself within the power structure of a historically white, male-dominated educational system—one that has been and continues to be influenced by systemic societal constructs.

Notes

1 Angelou, M. (1969). *I know why the caged bird sings*. Random House.
2 Jackson, J., & Shakeshaft, C. (2003, April 22). *The pool of African-American candidates for the superintendency* [Paper presentation]. American Education Research Association Annual Meeting, Chicago, IL, United States. https://files.eric.ed.gov/fulltext/ED479479.pdf, p. 13.
3 Jackson, J., & Shakeshaft, C. (2003, April 22). *The pool of African-American candidates for the superintendency* [Paper presentation]. American Education Research Association Annual Meeting, Chicago, IL, United States. https://files.eric.ed.gov/fulltext/ED479479.pdf, p. 12.
4 Alston, J. A. (1999). Climbing hills and mountains: Black women making it to the superintendency. In C. C. Brunner (Ed.), *Sacred dreams: Women and the superintendency* (pp. 79–90). State University of New York.
5 Taylor, T. S. (2007). Battling bias: It's still about race. But it's not in your face. *Essence*, *4*, 164–167, p. 165.
6 Blount, J. M. (1998). *Destined to rule the schools: Women and the superintendency 1873–1995*. State University of New York.
7 Jackson, J., & Shakeshaft, C. (2003, April 22). *The pool of African-American candidates for the superintendency* [Paper presentation]. American Education Research Association Annual Meeting, Chicago, IL, United States. https://files.eric.ed.gov/fulltext/ED479479.pdf.
8 Jackson, J., & Shakeshaft, C. (2003, April 22). *The pool of African-American candidates for the superintendency* [Paper presentation]. American Education Research Association Annual Meeting, Chicago, IL, United States. https://files.eric.ed.gov/fulltext/ED479479.pdf.
9 Bell & Chase, 1993, as cited in Alston, J. A. (2005). Tempered radicals and servant leaders: Black females persevering in the superintendency. *Educational Administration Quarterly*, *41*(4), 675–688; Björk, L. (2000). Introduction: Women in the superintendency—advances in research and theory. *Educational Administration Quarterly*, 36(1), 5–17.
10 Brunner, C. C., & Peyton-Caire, L. (2000). Seeking representation supporting Black female graduate students who aspire to the superintendency. *Urban Education*, 35(5), 532–548.

11 Fitzgerald, T. (2006). Walking between two worlds. *Educational Management Administration & Leadership*, *34*(2), 201–213.

12 Alston, 2000; Brown, 2014; Méndez-Morse, S. (1999). Redefinition of self: Mexican-American women becoming superintendents. In C. Cryss Brunner (Ed.), *Sacred dreams: Women and the superintendency* (pp. 125–140). State University of New York; Ortiz, F. I. (2000). Who controls succession in the superintendency? A minority perspective. *Urban Education*, *35*(5), 557–566; Revere, 1986, 1987; Rodriguez, 2014.

13 Brown, A. R. (2014). The recruitment and retention of African American women as public school superintendents. *Journal of Black Studies*, *45*(6), 573–593. https://doi.org/10.1177/0021934714542157.

14 Méndez-Morse, S. (1999). Redefinition of self: Mexican-American women becoming superintendents. In C. Cryss Brunner (Ed.), *Sacred dreams: Women and the superintendency* (pp. 125–140). State University of New York.

15 Méndez-Morse, 1999, p. 137.

16 Méndez-Morse, 1999, p. 137.

17 Méndez-Morse, 1999, p. 127.

18 Ortiz, F. I. (2000). Who controls succession in the superintendency? A minority perspective. *Urban Education*, *35*(5), 557–566.

19 Burton, L. J., Cyr, D., & Weiner, J. M. (2020). "Unbroken, but bent": Gendered racism in school leadership. *Frontiers in Education*, *5*. https://doi.org/10.3389/feduc.2020.00052.

20 Brown, A. R. (2014). The recruitment and retention of African American women as public school superintendents. *Journal of Black Studies*, *45*(6), 573–593. https://doi.org/10.1177/0021934714542157, p. 587.

21 Brown, 2014, p. 579.

22 Ortiz, F. I. (2001). Using social capital in interpreting the careers of three Latina superintendents. *Educational Administration Quarterly*, *37*(1), 58–85, p. 62.

23 Rodriguez, S. A. (2014). *Extraordinary women in Texas: A phenomenological study of Mexican American female superintendents* [Doctoral dissertation, Texas State University].

24 Alston, J. A. (2000). Missing from action: Where are the Black female school superintendents? *Urban Education*, *35*(5), 525–531.

25 Brown, A. R. (2014). The recruitment and retention of African American women as public school superintendents. *Journal of Black Studies*, *45*(6), 573–593. https://doi.org/10.1177/0021934714542157.

26 Burton, L. J., Cyr, D., & Weiner, J. M. (2020). "Unbroken, but bent": Gendered racism in school leadership. *Frontiers in Education*, *5*. https://doi.org/10.3389/feduc.2020.00052.

27 Alston, J. A. (2005). Tempered radicals and servant leaders: Black females persevering in the superintendency. *Educational Administration Quarterly*, *41*(4), 675–688.

28 Jean-Marie, G., Williams, V. A., & Sherman, S. L. (2009). Black women's leadership experiences: Examining the intersectionality of race and gender. *Advances in Developing Human Resources*, *11*(5), 562–581. https://doi.org/10.1177/1523422309351836, p. 573.

29 Dear Potential Candidates,

Your participation in a study on K–12 school superintendency/headship is requested. I am a doctoral student in the Department of Education Leadership and Policy at Hofstra University. I am conducting a qualitative study entitled: "A

Qualitative Study Examining Black Women's Accessibility to and Experiences in the Superintendent Pipeline." This qualitative study examines the intersectionality of race and gender as it relates to the exclusivity of the superintendency (head-of-school) pipeline and position. IRB approval from Hofstra University was obtained in the Summer of 2022.

For this study, I am interested in interviewing current Black women superintendents (heads of schools) in K–12 school settings. My goal: is to collect and report on the perspectives and experiences of Black women superintendents. I hope the information from this study will shed light on the barriers faced and give insight regarding strategies that can dismantle "*isms*" and break the *glass ceiling* for a more equitable superintendency pipeline.

Ultimately, knowledge from this research may inform recruiting firms, universities, schools, and aspiring Black women leaders, on ways to overcome and reform inequities in education executive leadership. Moreover, this study may also bring attention to an area that is underrepresented in research and may offer new theoretical lenses to examine the phenomenon.

I would like to invite you to participate in a one-on-one interview and focus group panel. I expect individual and focus group interviews will be approximately 50–60 minutes. I will keep the identity of all participants confidential in the report publication and presentation. The results of this study will be used for the educational purposes of the course and may be used to influence further research elsewhere.

With your consent, I would like to record Zoom interviews, so I have an accurate account of what we discuss. At any point during this study, you may reserve the right to speak off the record.

If you would like to participate in my research as an interviewee, please let me know some possible dates/times in February that would be convenient for you. I can be reached via email: nrichards1@pride.hofstra.edu, nadinerichards1973@gmail.com, or by telephone: at 718-753-0679.

I look forward to hearing from you. Thank you for your time and consideration.

Sincerely,

Nadine Richards

30 These questions were:

Do you work in an independent school? If yes, which one?

What is your role and how long have you been at your current school? What are your current role and employer?

What are the goals of your study? How would they benefit independent schools? Please provide a brief description of your study.

What is your timeline for the interviews and focus groups?

What additional data or information are you planning to include in your study?

Who else will have access to your study? How do you plan to disseminate your findings?

31 IRB approval was obtained prior to the data collection. Before each interview, interviewees were provided with a written informed consent form, as required by the Hofstra IRB, and they were reminded that they had the option to opt out of the study at any time.

32 McClellan, 2011, as cited in Suggs Mason, B. (2021). *Intersectionality and the leadership of Black women superintendents* [Doctoral dissertation, University of Illinois Urbana–Champaign], p. 90.

· 5 ·

PIONEERS' GRIT: CLAIMING SEATS AND STANDING STRONG

If they don't give you a seat at the table, bring a folding chair.

—Shirley Chisholm[1]

This chapter explores the challenges these pioneering women encountered on their paths to and during their tenure as superintendents or heads of schools. As the first Black women (or, in most cases, women of color or simply women) to hold such positions, their stories are testaments to perseverance, strength, and resilience—the grit that allowed them to overcome countless barriers. While hopeful about progress, they candidly shared the persistent barriers that continue to marginalize Black women, even as other marginalized groups in educational leadership have gained representation. This perception was corroborated by the document review, which revealed significant gaps and disparities in the existing research.

Institutional Erasure: Invisible and Missing Data

A review of superintendent/head demographic statistics, both state and national levels, revealed a lack of comprehensive data specifically on Black women. The underreporting and invisibility of Black women in the field were striking. The document analysis of national and New York State data supported the literature and participant interviews, revealing that national and state associations do not systemically collect demographic data on superintendents, particularly regarding race, gender, or the intersection of these identities.

Nonetheless, cross-analysis allowed for some descriptive statistics. For example, the NAIS's Data and Analysis for School Leadership (DASL) reports, which collects school leadership data by state and nationally, includes optional reporting on race and ethnicity. Table 3 presents the reported percentages of heads of school by race and gender. The actual numbers are excluded to protect the small demographic of Black women heads, including those who participated in this study. The data reveal that 1.7% of the heads in New York State independent schools are Black women, compared to 35% White women and 51% White men. This finding is consistent with scholarly research confirming that initiatives to increase women's representation in top leadership roles have disproportionately benefited White women.

Table 3 *NAIS' 2022–2023 New York State Heads of School Data Analysis for School Leadership Demographics by Race and Gender*

Race	Women	Men
Black	1.7%	N/A
White	35%	51%
BIPOC	8%	3.5%
Total Races Requested	44.7%	54.5%

Data from NYSCOSS, informally collected every 3–5 years, provides a limited snapshot of the racial and gender diversity among New York State public school superintendents. Table 4 illustrates available data the agency had of New York State public school superintendents by race and gender. As shown in the accompanying table, the data lacks a breakdown of the broader BIPOC category, making it difficult to ascertain the precise representation of specific racial groups among superintendents. Therefore, it is not possible to

Table 4 *NYSCOSS 2022–2023 NYS Public School Superintendents by Race and Gender*

Race	Women	Men
Black	2.4%	2.4%
White	21.4%	N/A
BIPOC	3.4%	N/A
All Races Represented (by gender)	27.2%	72.6%

determine the exact percentage of Black women superintendents in New York state public schools based on this data alone. Despite the lack of complete data, the available information paints a clear picture: Black women represent about 2.4% of superintendents in New York State public schools. While the exact figures for other racial and gender groups might be uncertain, it's evident that White women (21%) and White men (presumed to be the vast majority, over 70%), significantly outnumber Black women in these leadership roles. This stark contrast underscores the persistent dominance of White males in educational leadership, highlighting a significant diversity gap that warrants attention and further investigation. This finding aligns with scholarly research confirming White male dominance in educational leadership Nonetheless, it is important to note that this data excludes New York City superintendents but includes BOCES and Special Act superintendents, which could influence the overall representation figures. Additionally, the limitations of the NYSCOSS data, particularly the lack of disaggregation for the BIPOC category, warrant cautious interpretation of the findings.

Brunner warned that "the underrepresentation of women and persons of color in superintendent-head positions remains significant."[2] Now, more than two decades later, Black women's representation in these leadership roles remains disproportionately low. For example, in the 2022-2023 AASA National Superintendent Salary and Benefits Survey, of with 2,435 respondents sharing their race and gender, Black women represented less than 1.8% of U.S. public school superintendents (see Table 5). This figure aligns with Revere's earlier research and indicates a persistent stagnation in the number of Black women attaining superintendencies.

Table 5 *AASA 2022–2023 Superintendent Salary and Benefits Survey Results: U.S. Public School Superintendents by Race/ Ethnicity*

Race/Ethnicity	Female	Male	Total
White (not Hispanic or Latino)	556	1,614	2,170
Black or African American	43	51	94
Hispanic or Latino Asian	24	49	73
Native Hawaiian or other Pacific Islander	1	3	4
American Indian or Alaska Native	4	11	15
Two or more races	7	20	27
Prefer not to answer	5	30	34
Other	5	12	16
Total	645	1,783	2,435

Similarly, the 2022–2023 DASL survey of independent school heads in the U.S. (Table 6), with 995 respondents providing data on race and gender, shows only a slightly higher representation of Black women at 4.1% and Black men at 2.3%. In stark contrast, White women comprise 37% of respondents, indicating that even within a patriarchal, male-dominated society, race appears to be a significant factor in superintendent acquisition or retention. These findings underscore the enduring challenges faced by Black women in accessing and advancing to top leadership positions in education, despite decades of awareness and initiatives aimed at increasing diversity. Furthermore, the data suggests that while gender plays a role, race remains a significant compounding barrier to attaining and maintaining superintendent positions.

Table 6 *NAIS 2022–2023 DASL Survey Disaggregated by Independent U.S. School Heads' Race and Gender*

U.S. Heads of School by Race: 2022–2023	Female	Male	Other	Total
Asian	11	6		17
Black/African American	41	33		74
Middle Eastern	4			4
Native Hawaiian/other Pacific Islander	1			1
Race not listed	4	6		10
Two or more races	14	9		23
White	369	495	2	866
Grand total	444	549	2	995

Additionally, the analysis of the available data suggests an incomplete picture. It reveals the need for more systematic and intentional collection of superintendent demographic data. The disparity noted aligns with the concept of intersectionality, as articulated by Kimberlé Crenshaw, which posits that Black women often face unique forms of discrimination due to the overlapping systems of racism and sexism.

Crenshaw argued that due to their race and gender, Black women are often legally and socially unprotected unless their experiences coincide with those of White women or Black men.[3] When researchers do not take this into account, Black women are forced to fit into the constructs of either the dominant culture of White men superintendents or the marginalized dominant groups of White women (privileged by their race) and Black men (often privileged by gender). These theoretical frameworks are reflected in the lived experiences of Black women in educational leadership.

Dr. Le Labo shared an incident from early in her career, highlighting this disparity between the representation of Black women and White individuals in educational leadership positions. Invited to a social benefit at the home of a prominent parent and business owner, she was directed to "go around the back" by the doorman. Fortunately, another parent coming into the elevator intervened, recognizing her and said, 'Oh no. This is Dr. Le Labo," correcting the doorman's discriminatory assumption.

This incident underscores the unique challenges faced by Black women in educational leadership, as their intersecting identities can lead to microaggressions, biases, and assumptions that hinder their advancement and recognition. The data further supports this, indicating that Black women's experiences in these roles often differ from those of White women. As Ms. Chanel noted, "For Black women… our tolerance for pain is so much higher… It's terrible for us, but schools certainly benefit from it… the only way out is through."

The personal accounts and statistical evidence converge to highlight the need for systemic change in educational leadership. Standing up to and dismantling these systemic issues benefits every member of the community. Dr. Valentino noted that in predominately White institutions like independent schools, structural racism need to be navigated and resolved, especially for Black women who experience these issues both professionally and personally. Valentino explained the unique burden shouldered by Black women in leadership:

> These institutions [independent schools] exist within our society and so there are aspects of bias and structural racism that you will be called to navigate to try to solve, at the same time that as a Black woman [you] are experiencing those things within society, potentially within the school as well. So, you're called to be in it and also to be taking care of it at the same time in a way that I think is unique.

Valentino's words highlight a central paradox of this study: Black women superintendents/heads experience both sexism and racism. While navigating these multidimensional, intersecting systemic oppressions, Black women leaders are simultaneously expected to use their power and positionality to dismantle these very barriers.

This paradox is evident in the personal accounts shared by participants. For example, Ms. Chanel recalled a disheartening incident on her last day at a school before assuming a new leadership role elsewhere. Instead of offering congratulations and well wishes, her predecessor and former boss told her, "You're not going to make it out there." This blatant attempt at gaslighting and undermining her confidence could have been demoralizing. However, Ms. Chanel transformed this negativity into motivation. When the opportunity presented itself, she returned to that same school to replace her former head, defying the prediction and proving her resilience, all while navigating the challenges of new motherhood. Similarly, Dr. Le Labo was motivated when she was overlooked. She recalls that as an assistant superintendent she did all the work, including teacher negotiations and curriculum alignment, at a time when this was not part of the educational landscape even in the best schools. Yet, her contributions were often minimized or dismissed. Dr. Le Labo recalls a pivotal moment when she was left waiting to be called into an executive board meeting, only to discover later that the meeting had concluded hours earlier without her input.

> I was in my office and [my superintendent] was holding an executive session with the board and he said, 'OK, I'm going to speak with the board. And when I'm ready to call you in to explain'—because he could never explain what I had done—'When I'm ready, I'll call you in, and you can explain what we came up with.' So, I was in my office... the session started at 8 o'clock. And usually, things go late. So, around 11:30 pm, the custodian came into my office and he said, 'Dr. Le Labo, aren't you going home?' ... I said, I'm waiting for the board. I'm waiting to be called in for the board.' He said, 'They left 2 hours ago.' He forgot to call me. And I was reading *Education Week* and the job for [superintendent] was right there. And those were my signs... Never would've applied had this not occurred. And the rest is history.

Dr. Le Labo realized that she was not only capable of doing the job, but was already doing it yet she was being consistently overlooked. She states, "I was pushed. How dare... I had become such a fixture that I was like the furniture. Always dependable, always there, always left." This realization spurred her to seek out and ultimately secure a superintendent position, turning a painful experience into a catalyst for her career advancement.

Courage, strength, and perseverance resonated with all participants. Dr. Valentino eloquently captured the symbolic power of Black women in leadership positions:

> There's a symbolic aspect to it as well. When you look at structural racism and you look at structural sexism and things of this nature, I think to see a Black woman in this role is to have an institution that is posing a counter-narrative to the more limited narratives that have sometimes been ascendant in our society.

It is critical for school communities and stakeholders to see Black women superintendents/ heads beyond the narrow definitions that society frequently perpetuates. Likewise, in building relationships with these varied stakeholders, it is important to stand up and speak out against discrimination, microaggressions, and biases.

Many participants shared experiences in which they had to confront such biases directly, often calling others into growth. Dr. Le Labo, the first woman and first Black person to lead in the predominantly White school district, recounted a powerful encounter with a board member who was disrespectful towards her and other women:

> And one day, my first year there, he was just really nasty. I mean, unbelievably nasty. And I looked him in the eye and I said, "There's something about me that you're not going to change. One is I'm never not going to be a woman." Because he was very disrespectful to women. "And I'm never not going to be Black. So, what are we going to do?"

This bold confrontation, during her very first year as superintendent, led the board member to question whether she was accusing him of racism. Dr. Le Labo's response was both firm and direct:

> I'm not accusing you. I'm just telling you. I'm not going to change being Black, and I'm not going to change being a woman. So, let's see.

Dr. Le Labo, an outspoken and courageous leader, revealed her penchant for "good spars," meaning the willingness to engage in difficult conversations and stand up for what is right. What bothered her was not just his personal mistreatment, but also the abusive behaviors she witnessed him repeatedly direct at female Jewish board members, which others saw but failed to address or stop. So, Dr. Le Labo took a stand, and recited the poem "They Came for the Jews" in the middle of the board meeting to highlight the interconnectedness of all forms of oppression.

This act of defiance solidified her support within the community. Dr. Le Labo explains:

> Nobody had the gumption to stand up... And he kept going on and being abusive and at a board meeting one night... I read the poem... And after I did that... there was nothing I could do that was wrong. Because I defended her. And so, I had the parents, I had the faculty, and I had three board members solidly behind me. And you know what? He lost the election the next time around. I survived him.

"Good spars," for Dr. Le Labo, signifies the inner will or fortitude required to fight against injustices and stand up for what is right. It demonstrates courage in the face of opposition and a resolve to speak out against wrongdoing despite potential risks or repercussions. By defending the Jewish woman, Le Labo's demonstrated to the community that she is a fighter committed to ethics and justice, confirming the interconnectedness of all forms of injustice. Her actions exemplify how individuals can take action to promote justice even if they aren't personally harmed. Essentially Dr. Le Labo's story exemplifies how confronting injustice head-on can not only protect the vulnerable but also galvanize support and ultimately lead to positive change.

The experiences of other participants echoed similar themes of resilience and defiance. Dr. Dior, an ordained Pentecostal minister who embraced her unique style, recounted during a superintendent board meeting being told she couldn't sit in a seat reserved for Jewish rabbis. Her response was simply, "Who said? Really? Move over." "You become relevant, not accidentally... on purpose, by design, because you're supposed to be there," Dr. Dior asserted. This assertive stance resonated with women in the community who often felt voiceless, solidifying Dr. Dior's position as a leader willing to challenge the status quo. They saw her as a woman who was outspoken, strong, and unapologetic.

These narratives also shed light on the gendered and racialized expectations that create barriers for women, particularly Black women, in educational leadership. Participants also talked about how gender roles and stereotypes create organizational, structural, and self-imposed barriers. In a leadership field in which maleness and Whiteness have prevailed for centuries, it influences systems and structure. Men, White men particularly, move differently in and throughout the educational leadership landscape. For example, "if men are not ready for the job, they go for the job anyways," Dr. Fenty stated. Similarly, Dr. Ambrosia added, "There's research that shows that White men can go right from the principalship and become superintendents. Women spend a lot more time in central office roles, helping men lead districts."

Moreover, participants shared that women tend not even to apply for a leadersip job unless they feel they are overqualified. In contrast, Dr. Le Labo asserts, men will apply for a superintendency before they are ready for one. Women, on the other hand, "have to be overcooked. They have to be well done, have explored everything, completed everything, and checked all the boxes before they will apply." This, she explained, "already takes them out of the journey." While this is the case for women in general, "Women of color even more so because they tend to know that they're good assistants." This discrepancy, combined with the persistent stereotypes associated with age and gender, creates a complex landscape for women aspiring to leadership, especially women of color.

Some of the participants thought that in addition to gender stereotypes, there were age stereotypes for younger (or younger-looking) female heads and superintendents. In contrast, a younger man assuming a superintendency/headship is perceived in a more favorable light. For men, youth is seen as an asset, whereas for women youth is perceived as a deficit.

The age factor triples the biases for Black women, whose race and gender already offer oppressive stereotyping. Dr. Ambrosia shared that as a Black woman, she felt people perceived her young appearance as a disqualification and "underestimated what I knew and what I could do." She elaborated:

> We have been trained by the system to internalize our own oppression in ways that we do not see us as being competent, credible... I just don't feel like we have internalized that a Black woman with an Afro, bushy hair, and brown skin can be my boss. I think we have not gotten there yet.

Ms. Chanel added that these barriers can also be internalized and self-imposed:

> Initially, I was my biggest barrier because what I've seen is White men do this job by and large or White women do this job by and large... So, first was just, I didn't see myself doing it.

Dr. Ambrosia added:

> I think there's still a lot of gender roles that make us feel guilty for the choices that we make to pursue leadership... It's important to invest in all of our relationships, but it's almost like, "Oh, you're a wife and ain't here. You're not home."... Whereas I never hear anyone tell my male counterparts, "You're never home."

Despite advanced degrees, preparation, and experience, Black women heads and superintendents with intersecting race, gender, and age identities believe they are frequently challenged by members of their community in ways that men of any race or White women are not. Ms. Chanel, who was 40 when she first entered her headship, shared:

> I feel like people feel far more comfortable challenging me professionally than they would anyone else of another background, but I think certainly men of any race and a lot of times White women too. White women sometimes being the leaders of some of

> those challenges coming up, where there are many times over the past year where I've thought I could not imagine fixing my face to say that to someone who was my actual boss. And there are ways that we could talk about the issue here, that are not being presented in a way that is actually disrespectful to me. I think about that and just the stress that comes with having to deal with the way that people can speak to me.

Similarly, Dr. Ambrosia recounted being second-guessed and even having her dissertation quoted back to her. She said, "I've had people Google me and read my dissertation and quote it back to [me]. And it's almost like a constant need to affirm that I earned this. I don't know why that is."

The superintendents and heads who had been in their roles longer seemed to have overcome these challenges. At age 73, Dr. Dior said she now uses her voice in ways she may not have earlier in her career: "You get to the point where you stand up... That's where I am right now. I am almost repenting for the time that I couldn't or didn't." Dr. Le Labo a superintendent for 17 years who has won many awards and public recognitions for her work, described her approach to microaggressions:

> The thing is, I really was in command... about my superintendency... I don't get that garbage. They don't throw those [microaggressions] at me... Newsday uses me as an authority on the matter... I'm in the room. I'm in the room where it happens, and I make myself available to be in the room where it happens. So, I don't feel barriers... I'm sure they're there, but I choose not to see them. I tunnel through them.

Perhaps the discrimination and biases still exist, but these women's confidence and accomplishments allow them to push past them.

Many participants alluded to their humble, and even impoverished upbringing, where class and poverty were perhaps the first barriers they faced. Education and a love of learning became the path to overcome race and gender and age-based obstacles. Due to these intersecting identities, these Black women leaders faced systemic and historical challenges, as well as structural ones inherent in how schools operate.

Structural and Organizational Deterrents

Many participants identified structural and organizational components of the superintendency/headship that disproportionately challenge Black women. Two primary issues emerged: the all-consuming nature of the role and the limited access to operational experience for many women, especially Black women.

Dr. Valentino described the role's demands:

> I almost can't express how all-consuming the role is ... People often will say, "Oh, I'm glad I'm not you" because you're always both trying to work proactively and also responsibly often to novel ... So, it takes up a tremendous amount of one's physical, mental, and emotional energy. I think it's important to know that before going into headship ... In so many ways what we're doing is an extension of what we've done in the classroom ... just with a greater amount of intensity.

The traditional pathway to the superintendency often favors secondary principalships, and participants noted that the operational side of education—facilities, finance, legal, technology—is an area where many women leaders lack experience. Dr. Ambrosia explained:

> I think that there's still a lot of bias around what the chief executive officer... should and could look like... There's still an extreme amount of bias. And a lot of unconscious bias that weeds people out of the process early. I think that there's a lot of research on our pathway to leadership. So even though you have to have a very strong instructional vision, there are a lot of operational pieces and legal pieces, and financial pieces that you also have to be responsible for. And we are capable of all of that; however, the majority of women, period, Black, White, Latinx, and Indigenous, the majority of women in education, are elementary school educators. The majority of people that are assigned to the superintendency are secondary educators. And, let's say, you're an elementary principal, once you leave the principalship and you go into central office... if you are in a curriculum and instructional role, like an assistant superintendent of curriculum, the likelihood is that you will [still] not be exposed to some of the operational pieces that you need to be competent and fluent in order to be a successful superintendent.

Dr. Valentino concurred, noting that even with her experience as an upper school director, she would have benefited from "more grounding in finance." As a head of school, she had to be a quick study of the financial and operational sides of the role. Dr. Valentino's exposure to admission enrollment and her secondary leadership role offered some preparation into the operational side of the headship/superintendency role but not at the breadth needed. Dr. Ambrosia wondered whether "on some level, there's a little gatekeeping going on,... conscious or unconscious, [Black women] just have a lack of opportunity to get that experience."

Dr. Valentino also elaborated on the importances of these competencies:

> So, you can have the most amazing vision for leadership, and you could be really great in curriculum instruction, but by and large, the board of education wants to know, can you protect our money? Do you know how to safeguard our resources? Do you understand what to do in a time of crisis? And again, I know that we can, but I think that we don't always get the same experiences as our male counterparts, who are [often] secondary educators.

Interestingly, all six study participants had exposure to the operational leadership and/or were secondary division leaders/principals. Ms. Chanel worked in fundraising and advancement. Dr. Valentino was a secondary principal and worked in admissions. Dr. Dior was not considered or offered a superintendency until she transferred from elementary to secondary leadership. Dr. Le Labo had advanced degrees and expertise in mathematics and science and worked significantly in secondary leadership. Dr. Fenty had a bachelor's degree in marketing, and Dr. Ambrosia was a founding principal of a high school.

This underscores the importance of such experience in overcoming systemic barriers and suggests that incorporating operational components into superintendent preparation program could be a viable strategy to address these obstacles proactively. These women's accounts offered some insights into other deterrent that can be restructured within the scope of the role to be more inclusive and supportive of Black women in the headship and superintendency.

Interviews and document analysis revealed a significant structural-operational barrier: salary disparities. These disparities affected independent heads of schools and public school superintendents differently, with the latter being more negatively impacted. Heads of independent schools generally earn double the salary of public school superintendents, yet salary gaps persist across both sectors, with White men and men of color often earning more than Black women. For example, a 2021 report on Long Island public school superintendent salaries revealed that Black women superintendents earned less than their White female and male counterparts of all races. In the Garden City Patch article, Alex Costello reported that the highest-paid public school superintendent salary on Long Island was $334,000, with benefits totaling $421,499 in total compensation. This job was held by a White woman. The highest-compensated superintendent, a man of color, had a total salary and benefit package of $455,572.[4]

Overcoming Barriers: The Importance of Support Systems

The participants attributed their success in securing and thriving the superintendent/head role to the resources and support in their lives. Both informal and formal networks proved invaluable. Informal support systems, such as friends, family, and professional networks, were cited by all participants. Some individuals benefited from formal networks like search firms, consultants, therapists, and caregivers. Notably, those in independent headships may have also benefited from higher salary compensation, a potential advantage not afforded to public school superintendents. These combined informal and formal networks served as crucial social capital, empowering participants to overcome barriers, access leadership positions, and navigate the unique challenges they encountered.

Faith, family, and friends emerged as vital pillars of strength and support for these leaders. All participants shared how their faith and belief systems significantly influenced them. For instance, Dr. Dior commented, "I am excited about my walk and my role. The one thing that's significant about me is that I am an ordained licensed minister, and my faith is my work and my work is my faith." Similarly, Dr. Ambrosia added, "I have my church community that prays for me and encourages me."

Alongside their faith, family also played a crucial role, particularly for those with younger children. Ms. Chanel, a mother of two young children, emphasized the essential role her husband and caregiver play in her success:

> I'm married, so I have a partner at home. And he's incredible in all ways as a parent and as a partner, and we can't do what we need to do professionally without the help of our caregiver... And I get frustrated because I feel like a lot of these conversations with women talking about how to manage this, they don't talk about the aspect of having somebody who does those things for you.

Dr. Ambrosia also shared the unwavering support she receives from her family:

> Even though I'm not home, they still remember me. So, I think that is my first line of defense and support. I have a very supportive husband... for me, just knowing that I can share the ups and downs of my... being able to share that is very important. And I have that, not just in my spouse, but I have my siblings, thank God, I have my parents. I actually also have two living grandparents. So multiple ways... folks that I know are loving me.

The Sisterhood: An Indispensable Lifeline

Beyond family and friends, all the participants spoke about the importance of their "sisterhood" networks of Black women or women of color. These networks provided support and a safe space for sharing experiences, challenges, and triumphs. While having family and faith-based support systems was important to all participants, the sisterhood emerged as an indispensable lifeline.

Dr. Le Labo, who found her "sister-friends" through her social circle and among educated peers, shared:

> So, I'm not a sorority person because my culture doesn't have that. But my church... I had that. I had a cadre of friends who were, I call them, sister-friends... we share our sorrows and griefs and wonderful experiences... And I always say, "That's my true family." My sister-friends are my true family. I would do anything for them. They would do anything for me... I can always call on them.

Echoing similar sentiments about the Black women friends and connections, Ms. Chanel emphasized the sustaining power of her network:

> [The] network that I already had of women of color, but explicitly Black women who are either senior administrators or other heads of schools, who I can reach out to at any time, who get it without a doubt and don't need an explanation and aren't going to try to Pollyanna me into anything, but can have the moments of like, 'girl, you better go do it,' or 'that is trash, don't mess with it.' And just affirming what I might know or encouraging me when I need that, all of that makes a huge difference.

Dr. Valentino, like the other participants, shared how her sisterhood of Black women heads had been an invaluable resource, providing immense support throughout her career: "I have gotten a tremendous amount of support from the relationships developed in those communities." She clarified that not all the Black women in her sisterhood circle were fellow heads of schools; some held different positions within education, while others worked in completely unrelated fields. Yet they consistently offered support and a "good ear." She elaborated:

> There's always a listening ear if you want to run something past them... that's been helpful as well. And then good friends who are either in the independent schools and clearly understand what [I'm] navigating [as well as others] who are in other fields... just Black women friends who know what I'm talking about.

Other participants spoke of the importance of their sisterhood, particularly during the COVID-19 pandemic and racial reckoning following George Floyd's murder. These coalitions of "sisters" provided crucial encouragement and understanding. Dr. Ambrosia mentioned the unique support she received from her colleagues of color:

> I do have colleagues that I can share with, particularly my colleagues of color, because... they understand the multiple layers of race, gender, leadership... We have text chains, and we go to conferences and we just try to share and encourage each other, because [the job] can be very isolated.

During the focus group discussion, I was able to observe the bond, trust, and relationship firsthand. Despite varying levels of familiarity, all participants felt a deep connection as they shared their experiences and journeys. Throughout the session, nonverbal cues and gestures like head nodding and flashing screens affirmed each other's comments, fostering an environment of validation and support. Words like "preach," "uhum," and "she told them" served as affirmations throughout the hour-long discussion.

The profound importance of the "sisterhood" for these Black women leaders aligns with Ortiz's research on social capital, discussed in Chapter 4 of this book. The strong bonds formed within these networks, often rooted in shared experiences, cultural understanding, and a sense of kinship, create a unique form of social capital that provides invaluable support, guidance, and validation. These sisterhoods serve as a counterbalance to the isolation and marginalization often experienced by Black women in educational leadership, offering a safe haven for navigating the challenges and celebrating the successes inherent to their roles.

Mentorship and Advocacy for Leadership Advancement

In addition to these informal support systems, participants cited formal professional networks and resources as instrumental in their career trajectories. Mentors, headhunters, search consultants, and supportive board members played crucial roles as "gatekeepers," advocating for and providing access to the superintendency and headship roles.

Dr. Valentino credited various mentors throughout her journey who supported her learning and helped pave a pathway to the headship. She acknowledged the numerous mentors, both Black and White, who recognized her potential and championed her success. Importantly, she noted that mentors need not be in superior positions; the qualification for mentorship lies in the ability to guide and inspire, regardless of title or hierarchy. Dr. Valentino recounted her experience with various mentors, sharing:

> I also was well mentored... My role models in this work have often been Black women, like for instance my first teacher is someone who I always invoke at this time of year in talking to my community. She wasn't the head of school; she was a classroom teacher in primary school, but she just had all of the things that you need to internalize. And so, I really admire that. My own mother also.

She further elaborated on the nature of mentorship, explaining:

> I will say this, there is a Black woman whom I adore who I ended up being her supervisor as I advanced in the field... She was always also a great mentor to me in terms of just thinking about how to support teams... She's always been a good ear as well. So mostly women; a few Black women and a few White women... I think in terms of actual mentorship, I was very heavily and I think expertly mentored by a White woman who really saw me and said, "I see you as a head of school some day," and said to my mother, "I see your daughter as a head of school some day."

Beyond mentorship, advocacy emerged as a significant factor in the participants' career progression and success. In particular, the influence of search consultants and school boards was highlighted as pivotal in providing access and opportunities for Black women to secure leadership positions.

Both independent school heads in the study emphasized how search firms and their consultants actively championed their candidacy for their current roles. These consultants and boards serve as gatekeepers, wielding significant influence in determining who gains access to these top executive positions. They play a crucial role in not only securing the positions but also fostering an environment conducive retention and success.

Dr. Valentino shared her experience with a supportive board, emphasizing the positive impact it had on her leadership:

> I have benefited from having a very strong, thoughtful, and appropriate board... I'm really grateful for that. And I also have a very close relationship with board members and in particular with the leadership of the board. We've gone on retreats together to think about how we can work together in service to the school.

This collaborative approach, involving retreats and open communication, fostered a strong partnership between Dr. Valentino and her board, ultimately contributing to her success and longevity in the role. Other participants echoed similar sentiments.

Additional Resources: Therapy and Compensation

In addition to these gatekeepers and professional networks, participants who held independent schools head positions also mentioned therapists and their salaries as resources that supported their retention and success. Therapists and other mental health professionals provided a valuable resource for self-care and well-being, given the unique challenges faced by Black women in leadership roles.

Futhermore, the financial aspect as a resources for support cannot be overlooked. Ms. Chanel's highlighted the significance of a high enough salary to afford childcare and other support services, allowing her to balance her professional responsibilities with her personal life. She explained:

> It's really important to me to say that I have a job with a high enough salary that allows me to pay someone well to do that work well for us in our home. That is the game-changing factor, hands down.

She further elaborated on how her salary supports her needs as a parent and allows her to afford a caregiver who helps to manage the traditional gender roles of housekeeping and childcare.

> It was 1,000%, my caregiver... can't do what we need to do professionally without the help of our caregiver. We have somebody who comes to our house each day who's there with my son, who picks up my daughter from school or will drop her off if that's necessary with different programs she's doing over the summer, who takes care of a lot of household tasks that take up a lot of time. There is no way that I would be able to survive without that.

Ms. Chanel's emphasis on the necessity of a caregiver, made possible by her salary, underscores the vital role that adequate compensation plays in enabling Black women to not only attain leadership positions but also sustain them. This highlights how salary and compensation, as a source of formal support, seem a notable factor specific to independent school heads that warrant further exploration. Her experience highlights how financial resources can alleviate the burdens often associated with traditional gender roles and create a more equitable foundation for success in demanding roles like the superintendency or headship.

A review of salaries revealed that independent school heads in New York earn upwards of $500,000 annually, and some salaries exceeded $1,000,000 annually. While, Black women independent school heads typically earn less than White men, most White women and men of color heads, their salaries still surpass those of New York public school superintendents.

Notably, Dr. Dior, a public school superintendent, mentioned that she was still paying off student loans for her doctorate. This anecdote highlights the financial challenges that many Black women leaders face, even after achieving significant career milestones. Addressing these inequities in compensation and providing adequate resources for professional development and personal support are crucial steps toward ensuring the retention and advancement of Black women in educational leadership.

Black Women Leaders Redefining Education

This chapter's title, Pioneers' Grit: Claiming Seats and Standing Strong delves into how intersectionality empowers Black women in their superintendent/head positions, enabling them to celebrate their uniqueness, overcome barriers, and cultivate more inclusive school communities. These pioneering leaders are innovative and driven, pushing boundaries to create positive change and advance equity. Their passion, courage, resilience, strength, and perseverance—what Angela Duckworth terms "grit"—are key to their success.[5]

Despite facing marginalization and oppression, these women emerge as trailblazers, demonstarting unwavering grit vital in acquiring and excelling in their positions. Their lived experiences emphasize empathy and equity, balanced with humility and confidence, which is evident in their interactions and the testimonials from others.

By promoting a better understanding of the multidimensional and unique lived experiences of Black women superintendents/heads within their societal context, this study provides an introductory profile—a HerStory—that captures their distinct spirit and grit. It reveals a hybrid identity that sets them apart from their racial and gender counterparts. The findings revealed that these participants are well-educated, well-prepared, have strong family ties, and are highly motivated by their support sysyems—formal and informal.

Intersectionality provided a critical lens to examine the marginalization these women experience, helping to understand the complex barriers they face. These include discrimination, microagressions, invisibiity, institutional erasure, and structural deterrents, all operating within a historical and socio-political framework that only intersectionality can fully explain.

Beyond Barriers: A Vision for Transformation

Beyond understanding these barriers and marginalization, these participants' testimonies provide hope and inform strategies for reform. Their hybrid identities are shaped by their commitment to making a positive impact and reforming the very systems that marginalize them. They leverage their intersectionality to build powerful coalitions, inviting gatekeepers and other stakeholders to join them in transforming schools for the betterment of humanity.

From these participants, we learn that the totality of identities is not the sum of their parts. Their distinct identity, formed from intersecting social categories, is a unique hybrid creation.[6] This study highlights the participants' pride in their Blackness, as exemplified by Ms. Chanel's declaration, "I am Black... regular Black... and happy for it!" This was a sentiment echoed by all. This pride was evident in their self-descriptions and their celebration of their natural hair as a "crown," challenging societal beauty standards and inspiring Black girls. There was a sense of empowerment that I observed and felt as I listened to these participants describe themselves.

Crenshaw's concept of "representative intersectionality," underscorces how self-perception and the perceptions of others are influenced.[7] The participants exercised agency in the politics of naming, modeling empowerment through their language. It's significant to note that various oppressed groups continue to use identity as a point of resistance. The phrases "I am Black" and "Black is beautiful" serve as powerful statements of self-identification, resistance, and affirmation, emphasizing the importance of reclaiming and celebrating diversity identities.

This study promotes a deeper understanding of these dynamics, highlighting the transformative leadership of Black women in education. Their unique experiences and hybrid identities not only reveal the challenges they face but also illuminate their potential to inspire change and lead effectively in diverse educational contexts.

Conclusion

The findings in this study align with existing literature indicating that Black women are often overqualified in comparison to their counterparts. That notwithstanding, these participants remained humble while knowing their worth.

Furthermore, the results highlight how intersectionality involves the intersection of Black (racial), female (gender), and superintendents'/heads' (role) identities, creating a unique group identity distinct from the individual social components. This research and its findings align with literature emphasizing the importance of an intersectional and Afrocentric lens for analyzing intragroups with multiple categories. The participants, Black women superintendents/heads, navigate a White male-dominated institution and society, critically examining the power structures in which they exist.

Despite their shared intersectional identities as Black women, systemic oppression introduced additional victimizing characteristics, such age, accent, hair, class, and marital status—which Carbado et al. referred to as "intra-intersectionality discrimination."[8] Ageism emerged as another social identity for two participants, Ms. Chanel and Dr. Ambrosia. Additionally, participants like Dr. Dior, Dr. Le Labo, and Dr. Valentino faced challenges related to classism and poverty in their childhood.

The literature questions the constructed nature of group identity boundaries and exposes how racialized and gendered oppression marginalizes and forces Black women to belong to a particular group.[9] These factors influence the participants' lives, decisions, and leadership styles. Their hybrid identity was composed of both immutable and mutable social constructs, operating fluidly across different context and time.

An intersectional perspective requires recognizing how power influences the application of social constructs. Yet considering social identity categories such as race or gender as neutral or independent of one another is incorrect. In contrast to merely identifying individuals by the social categories that may be used to define them, intersectionality acknowledges the unique social positions Black women hold.

Institutional Erasure and the Fight for Representation

This study highlights the institutional erasure Black women face in both public and private schools, limiting their access to superintendent/head roles and making their tenures difficult. All participants noted the low representation of Black women in these roles, corroborated by document review data and descriptive statistics. For example, a noteworthy finding is the extremely low number of Black women who led independent and public schools in New York State.[10] Similarly, fewer than 50 Black women superintendents were in the United States in 2000, and by 2022, there were only 41 Black women public school superintendents and 43 Black women heads according to AASA and NAIS, respectively.

The participants' experiences of discrimination, bias, gaslighting, and other harms due to their race and gender partly explain Black women's underrepresentation. They faced being overlooked, disregarded, put down, and undermined, with their qualifications often questioned. It was frequently difficult for the women to tell whether racial or gender bias was the source of the discrimination and microaggressions they encountered.[11] The erasure of Black women's gender, a crucial component of their intersectional identity, is deeply influenced by racialized perceptions of them.

Framing the experiences of Black women as a feminist issue contributes to further erasure. Although 26.4% of superintendents in U.S. public schools are women, only 1.7% are Black women. Similarly, when we look at all women in New York State independent schools, while 45.1% of heads are women, Black women comprise less than 2%. When we consider Black female superintendents' experience as a feminist one, we mistakenly conclude that progress is being made for all women.

The Need for Systemic Change

Sociohistorical awareness is essential for recognizing the root causes of various oppressive systems and privileges—and the ways in which they intersect.[12] Due to systemic institutional erasure, some participants internalized self-doubt, hesitating to pursue the superintendent or head position because they did not see people like them in these roles. This led to missed opportunities for advocacy and self-promotion, a result of learned systemic racist and sexist conditioning.

The organizational structure of the superintendency/headship roles, historically designed with male dominance in mind, perpetuates the stereotypical assumption that men are not primary caregivers. Thus, the demanding nature of these roles, with extremely long hours, can be challenging for women with caregiving responsibilities. Additionally, with the limited number of Black women superintendents and heads, locally and nationally, contributed to feelings of isolation among many participants.

Understanding how these women succeeded despite these challenges requires examining the support systems that helped them. Strong networks and resources played a critical role in overcoming barriers faced. Partcipants found strength in their faith, personal value systems, and family support, viewing these as a "first line of defense." Those who were married spoke highly of their supportive spouses. But it was the "sisterhood" of Black women that provided an invaluable community of shared common experiences and mutual support, essential for managing the stress of their roles and making difficult decisions.

The sisterhood offered microaffirmations, creating a safe space for authenticity and connection. A shared passion for making a difference in children's lives united the participants, who all emphasized the value of giving back and demonstrated a strong commitment to equity and inclusion. The focus group panel vividly showcased the camaraderie, affirmation, and validation that these relationships provided. It was powerful to watch.

Support also came from formal support networks, such as mentors and search consultants, who increased the participants' access to the superintendency/headship. Search consultants were gatekeepers who reached out to recruit and encourage their candidacy, playing a cruicial role in career advancement. Other resources, such as caregivers and therapists, supported participants' well-being and work-life balance. For example, caregivers offered essential resources for assisting with child rearing and meeting the traditional roles women play in society. Dr. Le Labo discussed how important this was for her early in her career. Likewise, Ms. Chanel, with two young children, was able to enter the headship role at a younger age while still raising children because of this resource.

All the participants shared stories of mentors whose sponsorship and advocacy put them in spaces where they could be seen. Sponsors, often White men provided access to networks and validation to acquire the role. Inspiringly, the public school superintendents with multiple superintendencies expressed a strong desire to mentor and sponsor aspiring leaders.

A Call to Action

The participants in this study built coalitions and employed transformative leadership, giving voice to and advocating for the best interest of students. They actively sought out mentors and sponsors, forging alliances to amplify their voices and access to opportunities. Clearly, Black women superintendents/heads are leaders capable of raising human consciousness, building meaning, and inspiring change. By embracing their perspectives and amplifying their voices, we can unlock the full potential of educational leadership and create schools that truly serve all students. Their commitment to social justice and equity, combined with their lived experiences and unique perspectives, positions them to challenge the status quo and create more inclusive and equitable educational environments.

Notes

1 Chisholm, S. (1970). *Unbought and unbossed*. Houghton Mifflin.
2 Brunner, C. C. (2008). Invisible, limited, and emerging discourse: Research practices that restrict and/or increase access for women and persons of color to the superintendency. *Journal of School Leadership*, *13*(4), 428–450. https://doi.org/10.1177/105268460301300405, p. 662.
3 Crenshaw, K. (1989). Demarginalizing the intersection of race and sex: A Black feminist critique of antidiscrimination doctrine, feminist theory and antiracist politics. *University of Chicago Legal Forum*, *1989*(1).
4 Costello, A. (2021). Long Island 2021 school superintendent salaries ranked. *Garden City Patch*. https://patch.com/new-york/gardencity/long-island-2021-school-superintendent-salaries-ranked.
5 Duckworth, A. (2016). *Grit: The power of passion and perseverance*. Scribner/Simon & Schuster.
6 Shields, S. A. (2008). Gender: An intersectionality perspective. *Sex Roles*, 59, 301–311. https://doi.org/10.1007/s11199-008-9501-8.
7 Crenshaw, K. (1991). Mapping the margins: Intersectionality, identity politics, and violence against women of color. *Stanford Law Review*, *43*(6), 1241–1299. https://doi.org/10.2307/1229039.
8 Carbado, D. W., Crenshaw, K. W., Mays, V. M., & Tomlinson, B. (2013). Intersectionality: Mapping the movements of a theory. *Du Bois Review*, *10*(2), 303–312. https://doi.org/10.1017/S1742058X13000349, p. 310.
9 Collins, 1989; Crenshaw, 1989, 1991; Moffitt, U., Juang, L. P., & Syed, M. (2020). Intersectionality and youth identity development research in Europe. *Frontiers in Psychology*, *11*, 78; Shields, 2008.

10 Actual figures will not be disclosed because doing so would make the study's participants clearly identifiable.

11 Crenshaw's intersectionality would suggest it is not an either-or situation. In fact, Crenshaw argued that looking at Black women's experiences as an either-or "fails to transcend differences... [and] ignores intragroup differences" (1991, p. 1242).

12 According to Godfrey, E. B., & Burson, E. (2018). Interrogating the intersections: How intersectional perspectives can inform developmental scholarship on critical consciousness. *New Directions for Child and Adolescent Development, 161*, 17–38.

· 6 ·

THE CALLING: HARNESSING INTERSECTIONALITY AS A SOCIAL MOVEMENT

When I dare to be powerful—to use my strength in the service of my vision—then it becomes less and less important whether I am afraid.

—Audre Lorde[1]

Beyond the support they received, these women all shared a profound motivation: a calling that resonated deeply within each participant. This finding underscores how intersectionality serves as a call to action—a tool for reform that urges societies into growth, dismantles systemic oppression against Black women, and advocates for greater inclusivity and social justice.

All the participants expressed a deep passion for equity, inclusion, and social justice work. They viewed their role as a calling, driven by their experiences and understanding of marginalized perspectives. These Black women leaders, following in the footsteps of trailblazers like Harriet Tubman, Sojourner Truth, and Shirley Chisholm, provide hope and direction for aspiring future leaders. Like escaping slaves guided by the North Star, these leaders courageously challenge injustice and strive for freedom. Dr. Le Labo articulated this sentiment:

> The North Star is about engaging meaningful work for kids and having them feel a sense of, kids or parents, have a sense of belonging. So, it's about sound instruction. It's about safe spaces for kids and families and making sure they have successful trajectories. Any place I've ever been, there's my imprint.

Dr. Le Labo emphasized the importance of nurturing future leaders, stating that with over a decade of experience, her calling was to mentor and sponsor others. She remarked:

> Growing that cadre of leaders, making certain... to mentor and support people in order for them to become... Anybody with the assistant in front of them is not a permanent role. Principals I could see being principals. But if you have an assistant in front of your name, it's not a permanent role; it means that you're serving somebody or you're doing somebody's work and that you need to do your own work. And I say it even to the people who worked for me. So, it's not that I'm pushing them out the door, but if you're really good, you need to have your own principalship or superintendency.

Dr. Le Labo pointed out the lack of encouragement for Black women, noting that they often do not receive the validation they deserve. She said:

> That's where I come in. My job is to seek them out and to let them know that they're ready... I see an obligation on my part to create the next leaders... and I took pride in knowing that there were six superintendents in the room that I had chosen at some point within my structure to hire and support. And they're now very successful superintendents.

The intersectional experiences of Black women superintendents and heads drive their North Star solutionist spirit to guide and lead change for the betterment of humanity. Crenshaw's perspective on intersectionality highlights its utility in reconciling the " the tension between assertions of multiple identities and the ongoing necessity of group politics."[2] Dr. Le Labo reflected on this notion, saying:

> The North Star is about engaging meaningful work for kids and having them feel... a sense of belonging... It's about sound instruction... safe spaces for kids and families and making sure they have successful trajectories.

Given the current societal landscape—marked by endemic racism, the global COVID-19 pandemic, and rapidly changing demographics—Black women superintendents and heads of school are needed more than ever. These leaders embody the roles of North Stars and tempered radicals, demonstrating a commitment to equity and care for children.

The Black women superintendents and heads in this study also exemplify the characteristics of "servant leaders," who prioritize relational collaboration and consensus-building, demonstrate strong efficacy, commit to the care of children, practice survival skills, and maintain a strong sense of spirituality and faith.[3] All participants spoke of a conscious connection to their faith, spirituality, and ancestors, which fueled their passion and commitment to not just their communities but humanity as well. Dr. Dior shared her experience:

> In this walk, each superintendent has to know if you are called… then you'll know, when that door opens, that's for you… When you say "a calling," I know that in 2008, my pastor said, "Sister Dior, stand up… God is calling you to be a superintendent." This was early in 2008. I hadn't thought about [it]. Really? No, Bishop, go ahead and preach, because I don't want you to get in trouble with the Lord. Sure enough, I started putting in those applications, and wow.

In the focus group, the following exchange illustrated a similar sentiment. Dr. Fenty asserted:

> There's a level of mindfulness, spiritualism, that is guiding and grounding us in our work. Even when Chanel is speaking about, she's quoting some of our ancestors, she's giving back to the ancestors… I'm talking about calling… There is, in our culture of who we are as women of color, this groundedness of spirituality that is allowing us to [be] steadfast in the calling that we've been asked to serve in.

Chanel added, "I'm going to tweak that just a little bit to say, not as women of color, but as Black women, because there's a difference there, too."

The study participants, as activists and "tempered radicals," facilitate change within their communities and beyond in a calm and inclusive manner. They work within the confines of their schools to advance changes that support marginalized individuals within the organization they are lead. Dr. Ambrosia emphasized:

> If the odds were so stacked against me and I was able to become a teacher and become a good teacher, and then become a principal, and then become eventually a good principal, then when I meet young people and families who feel broken or feel like the odds are stacked against them or other people have written them off… I know that it doesn't have to be that way. And so, my leadership journey is about ensuring that what is predicted doesn't turn out to be true.

When these women acquired their superintendency or headship, they did not accept the status quo. Rather, they used their dual insider-outsider perspective to build coalitions that set reform and change in motion. Ms. Chanel shared:

> I think just knowing that we can do it and knowing that it's our responsibility to bring other Black women and Black folks into those spaces as well, that we can't let go of that part. We don't get to just take the job.

The sense of obligation and responsibility to the greater good and humanity was echoed in every interview and the focus group panel. Dr. Valentino stated, "We have a responsibility to students beyond the ones who are in our immediate care." Dr. Fenty explained this common theme:

> Part of the journey is about giving towards the greater good of the cause... In this case, in education, I want to make sure that I leave behind a cohort of up-and-coming leaders who are willing to do the work and are wise enough to learn from our stories and our successful journeys and the obstacles because the obstacles are great learning.

Moreover, Dr. Le Labo asserted, "Children cannot be what they can't see." These women made daily, impactful changes, using their positionality and leadership to give students a voice and broader understanding of the world. Dr. Ambrosia stated:

> I feel like children of color are under heard. And even in communities where people of color run the school district, we are not used to listening to our children. So, I think that there are students who feel like, because they had the opportunity to have a voice under my leadership that [has] served them well, as they moved on to college into other things. Essentially, these Black women heads and superintendents see their positionality as a calling to help to diversify the pipeline for school for the generation of students they serve by their representation in the role, as well as their leadership style to give young people (students) voice and agency.

Essentially, these Black women heads and superintendents see their positionality as a calling to help diversify the pipeline for future generations of students by their representation in the role, as well as their leadership style to give young people (students) voice and agency. As Alston notes, a key aspect of intersectionality is that Black women often find themselves in environments with inherent power imbalances, and they leverage that power—originally designed to marginalize them—to create constructive change.

As part of intersectionality, Black women are often placed in these environments with power differentials, and they use the power that is originally intended as a mechanism of oppression to be transformed into an effective vehicle for constructive change."[4]

Gatekeepers and the Pipeline

The participants also highlighted the important role of gatekeepers as key players promoting the inclusion of Black women in the superintendent/head pipeline. All acknowledged headhunters as gatekeepers who allow or deny access. For three participants, gatekeepers, like search consultants and headhunters, were essential in giving them access to the role. The other three implied they were blocked and had to forge their own path.

Part of the data analysis and triangulation for this study included observing workshops on intercultural competency in hiring and minority recruitment. These observations allowed me to see various stakeholders, including many gatekeepers, navigate the hiring process and learn best practices. This firsthand experience was crucial in understanding how biases and practices affect the recruitment and selection of candidates. I saw firsthand that many board members, heads, and consultants did not recognize their own blind spots when it came to résumé and candidate reviewing. These workshop exercises exposed blatant biases, where candidates were rejected based on race, gender, age, geographic location, university attended, and prior work experiences. The presenter emphasized that everyone has biases and without formal training, interviewers and search committees may inadvertently let their biases affect the screening and hiring processes.

The Power of Allies and Advocacy

Allies in the search and hiring processes can make a significant difference, often, serving as gatekeepers who open doors to senior leadership positions. This dynamic was particularly evident in the focus group discussion, where Dr. Fenty recalled an instance when a White, older gentleman on a search committee championed Dr. Dior's candidacy.

> When he said her name, everyone listened, and that goes back to allyship and who is your ally? We could say what it is, but it was a White, older gentleman who said her name, and I knew she was going to be in after that… And she did. I remember that. That was important for me, because I was like, "Is he really endorsing an African American woman?" It helped me to look at him from a different lens, as well, because so often in our field, getting back to… who's sponsoring? Who're your allies? Who's getting you to the next step?

Dr. Dior chimed in, "So, what you have to do is to create credible messengers so that your voice comes from another voice box." Ms. Chanel agreed, recounting advice she received:

> "You need to find your White man." Look for one, find one... White man who put her name into spaces and invited her to different places. I've got a gang of them myself now for different purposes, different times, different communities that utilize them. So, absolutely, knowing who people will hear, that you can say it until you're blue in the face and they can say it in passing, and all of a sudden, it's different.

Dr. Fenty affirmed, "That matters. They've seen your résumé before, they've even met you before, but now, because of who... Oh, you know what? Got it." As the other women spoke, Dr. Dior flicked her Zoom video on and off to express her agreement. She shared, "That's my amen, sister. You better preach." The panel discussion was filled with similar validations and affirmations.

With regards to search firm consultants, participants in the headship and superintendency made it their duty to engage with these consultants both before and after appointment. They positioned themselves as resources capable of recommending and bringing other Black women into the leadership pipeline. Dr. Le Labo stressed the need for boards and search consultants to do more:

> We've got to seriously work with school boards. School boards have to embrace that it's OK to expand their pipeline and include more seriously, try to match their population with the people who are in front of them. So, school boards need to do a lot of work and we have to work with search consultants so that they don't keep the same stable going, rotating them. And that they really do look in different places. They look at the HBCUs, we need to find ways to expand the sororities, fraternities, the organizations like NAPSI and ALICE, and all of these organizations that have people in them looking for work. It's amazing to me that they don't do that. So, those are the recommendations that I would say that they have to expand where they're looking. If you're looking in the same places, you're going to find the same worms.

Addressing the DEI Backlash

Some participants noted a concerning pullback or pullout from diversity, equity, and inclusion work. Alston raised the pertinent question that remains unanswered, "Are our research communities in educational leadership ready, in the thick of the battle, to fill the gap?"[5] The participants emphasized the responsibility of organizations like NAIS, the National School Boards Administration, and NYSCOSS to collaborate with school boards improve the representation of Black women in leadership. One participant bluntly warned:

> But this [critical race theory] and all this other thing has really thrown us for a loop. So, people are now... a little cowardice in trying to do things, but we're going to get back there because we're not stopping. We're not stopping!

The participants' believed in the urgent need for all stakeholders to partake and play a role in making schools more inclusive. In the spirit of Audre Lorde's call to embrace power in service of a vision, the participants' unwavering commitment to challenging the status quo and advocating for marginalized voices demonstrates the necessity for those in positions of privilege and power to act with similar courage. The true "calling" of educational leadership lies not merely in occupying a position of authority, but in actively utilizing one's privilege, positionality, and power to create a more inclusive and equitable landscape, where the beauty, brilliance, and resilience of Black women are nurtured and celebrated, and their voices are amplified to transform the educational landscape. The participants' capacity and aspiration to lead were deeply rooted in their history. Historically, Black women are often viewed as the "messiah or scapegoat" for the communities they serve.[6] The participants demonstrated a shared commitment to their qualities and identities. They viewed it as their responsibility not only to drive change but also to encourage those who have benefited from and served as gatekeepers of the existing power structures to take accountability. This included urging White men to mentor and sponsor Black women and encouraging gatekeepers and board trustees to undergo implicit bias and intercultural competency training. By fostering these relationships and encouraging proactive allyship, the participants aimed to create a more inclusive and equitable environment within educational leadership.

Notes

1 Lorde, A. (1984). The transformation of silence into language and action. In *Sister Outsider: Essays and Speeches* (pp. 40–44). Crossing.

2 Crenshaw, K. (1991). Mapping the margins: Intersectionality, identity politics, and violence against women of color. *Stanford Law Review, 43*(6), 1241–1299. https://doi.org/10.2307/1229039, p. 1296.
3 Alston, J. A. (2005). Tempered radicals and servant leaders: Black females persevering in the superintendency. *Educational Administration Quarterly, 41*(4), 675–688.
4 Lorde, 1984, as cited in Alston, 2005, p. 677.
5 Alston, J. A. (2005). Tempered radicals and servant leaders: Black females persevering in the superintendency. *Educational Administration Quarterly, 41*(4), 675–688, p. 685.
6 Scott, 1990, as cited in Alston, J. A. (2005). Tempered radicals and servant leaders: Black females persevering in the superintendency. *Educational Administration Quarterly, 41*(4), 675–688.

· 7 ·

BLACK FEMINIST LEADERSHIP THEORY: "ROSE FROM CONCRETE MODEL"

Did you hear about the rose that grew from a crack in the concrete? Proving nature's laws wrong, it learned to walk without having feet… by keeping it's dreams… Long live the rose that grew from concrete …

—Tupac Shakur, The Rose That Grew from Concrete[1]

In a world grappling with ongoing wars on multiple continents, persistent racial tensions, the devastating impacts of the global pandemics, and the disturbing overturning of significant landmark rights protections, Swindler's[2] concept of competing ideologies clashing with cultural assumptions becomes increasingly relevant. This calls for an epistemological framework that challenges systemic inequalities but also powerfully amplifies marginalized voices, especially those of Black women in executive school leadership.

From the lived experiences of these Black women leaders, a social justice leadership model emerges. The "Rose from Concrete Intersectional Model" is a theoretical framework that builds upon the principles of Black feminist theory and intersectionality. Notably, this model incorporates the principles of double consciousness, conflict resolution, equity, resistance and inclusivity. Drawing inspiration from Tupac Shakur's metaphor, the framework serves as both an analytical lens for understanding diverse perspectives and a catalyst for leadership intervention and development, challenging those in privilege to grow and become accountable.

Table 7 provides a detailed overview of this leadership framework, outlining key themes, subthemes, their theoretical underpinnings, and how they manifest in the lived experiences of Black women superintendents and heads of school.

Table 7 Navigating Barriers, Enacting Change: The Rose from Concrete Black Feminist Leadership (BFL) Framework

Theme	Subthemes	Key Takeaways	Theoretical Implications	Significant Statements
Resilience in the Face of Adversity	Overcoming Systemic Barriers Navigating Intersectional Challenges Drawing Strength from Sisterhood	Black women leaders demonstrate exceptional strength in overcoming institutional obstacles and the compounding effects of racism and sexism.	Connects to BFL and Intersectionality, emphasizing the unique challenges and resilience formed by intersecting identities.	"But I think for Black women, in particular, in the history that we have in this country, our tolerance for pain is so much higher in a way that schools benefit from…"
Systemic Erasure and Resistance	Marginalization in Practice Lack of Representation in Research	Black women's leadership is often overlooked or undervalued, both in practice and scholarship.	Extends BFL and Intersectionality by highlighting the systemic erasure of Black women's experiences and contributions.	"this is my voice…who's the one that's going to stand up and tell you what you should have known years ago?"

Table 7 Continued

Theme	Subthemes	Key Takeaways	Theoretical Implications	Significant Statements
Transformative Leadership	Activism and Advocacy Dismantling Systemic Inequities Building Coalitions for Change	Black women leaders enact change-oriented leadership focused on justice, equity, and dismantling oppressive structures.	Aligns with BFL's emphasis on social justice activism and aligns with Critical Race Theory's focus on systems of power.	"...[they] have to expand where they're looking. If you're looking in the same places, you're going to find the same worms."
External Support Systems	Importance of Allyship Expanding Search Strategies Targeted Leadership Programs Mentorship and Sponsorship	External factors influence black women's access to leadership, necessitating active support, broader recruitment strategies, and particular development programs.	Reinforces the BFL model's emphasis on systemic change and the need for allies and institutional transformation.	"...network that I already had of women of color, but explicitly Black women who are either senior administrators or other heads of schools, who I can reach out to at any time..."

The metaphor of a rose emerging from concrete symbolizes the resilience and strength of Black women school superintendents and heads. While concrete has conventionally symbolized something immutable and unyielding, concrete in this context represents the systemic barriers that Black women leaders in education face. Yet, like a rose pushing through, they demonstrate remarkable resilience, overcoming obstacles, resisting the status quo, and flourishing when given the necessary support.

Black women leaders demonstrate exceptional resilience and strength in a field historically and traditionally dominated by White men. Their unique experiences offer an authentic epistemological perspective on how they transform challenges into opportunities for growth, developing the traits needed to lead in complex times. They courageously advocate for diversity, equity, and inclusion from within the very systems that have historically oppressed them. Much like concrete, which combines diverse elements to form a strong and versatile material, Black women leaders embody multifaceted identities that intertwine gender, race, and positionality. Their resilience is forged and deepens over time as they navigate difficult circumstances.

The six narratives in this study mirror the experiences of countless exemplary Black women educators, many of whom may never hold formal leadership titles. Central to the untold stories of Black women in educational leadership, the Rose from Concrete Model functions as an Afrocentric epistemological framework and an intersectional lens. It unveils strategies for overcoming barriers, and acts as a catalyst for transformative activism, reshaping educational institutions from within.

In the realm of leadership as activism, the lack of comprehensive demographic data and research on Black women in leadership perpetuates their organizational erasure and systemic disparities. Robust research, like the foundational role of concrete, would provide the knowledge needed to dismantle these disparities and the exclusive status quo. A thorough investigation into the distinct challenges and triumphs of Black women leaders is essential. The absence of such data hinders policy development, rendering these leaders invisible and vulnerable to inequitable outcomes within the educational system due to systemic biases and insufficient support.

Central to this discourse is the elucidation of these women's experiences, encompassing microaggressions, systemic oppressions, the duality of double consciousness, the compounded jeopardy emanating from racism and sexism, organizational erasure, and uneven power dynamics. despite these challenges, these Black women rise like roses from concrete, demonstrate remarkable resilience and ability to thrive amidst adversity.

Within the educational domain, Black women leaders, much like the resilient rose blooming through concrete, thrive amid the very barriers constructed to impede them. Just as diverse elements that form durable concrete, these leaders draw upon a rich tapestry of experiences to cultivate unwavering resilience.

Embedded within their identity and sense of purpose, analogous to the binding capacity of cement in concrete, lies a distinctive hybrid identity. Their identities—comprising gender, race, and leadership— coupled with their strong sense of purpose coalesce their unique experiences into a journey of transformative leadership. Over time, these accumulated experiences foster resilience, much like aggregates strengthen concrete, increasing their stability and equip them with the acumen to adeptly navigate challenges.

For many Black women leaders, an unwavering faith in God often forms a foundation for their remarkable journeys. Their deep sense of calling, like roots pushing through concrete, infuses their leadership with purpose, guiding them through challenges with resilience. This alignment with faith reflects principles of servant leadership, transforming their roles into a commitment to service, advocacy, and dismantling systemic barriers. Their leadership, in turn, becomes a force for change, turning barriers into pathways of progress.

An essential aspect to these narrative is the interdependent "sisterhood" that exists among Black women leaders, akin to the nurturing relationship between a rose and its environment. Just as the rose draws nourishment from the soil, these leaders draw strength from familial, cultural, and mentorship networks. Crucially, the "sisterhood" functions as an insulation that covers, cushions, and safeguards against the external harms of microaggressions, gaslighting, racism, stereotypes, sexism, and institutional erasure that these Black women encounter in their lived experiences as superintendents and heads of school. This insulation serves as a protective barrier, much like a rose's stem provides support for its bloom. And like a rose's stem supporting its bloom, this network bolsters their individual and collective capacities to lead with resilience, authenticity, and purpose—not merely to survive but thrive in their demanding roles.

The "sisterhood" fosters solidarity, mirroring the symbiotic relationship between a rose and its environment. Just as a rose thrives with nourishment from the soil, Black women leaders draw strength from their networks. Further, this collective sustenance sisterhood, akin to a rose's stem supporting its bloom, furnishes affirmation, mentorship, and a strong sense of belonging. Within this sisterhood, a dynamic exchange of wisdom, solidarity, and support amplifies their influence, cultivating a fertile ground for their leadership to blossom.

The experiences of Black women leaders' are inextricably linked to their ancestral heritage, exemplified by figures such as Harriet Tubman and Sojourner Truth. These women, much like celestial North Stars, transcend time, their legacies guiding the path forward. Their commitment to justice, freedom, and equity instills hope and provides direction, not only for their sisterhood but also radiating outward to inspire others. Harriet Tubman's indomitable spirit, which led countless souls to freedom, and Sojourner Truth's resolute advocacy for truth and human rights stand as constant reminders of the transformative power of leadership grounded in integrity and resilience. Black women leaders, drawing strength from these ancestral guides, forge a legacy that continues to guide, uplift, and empower, lighting the way for a more just and equitable future.

Like the unfolding petals of a rose, Black women leaders bring multifaceted perspectives to leadership. Their lived experiences with racism and sexism inform a nuanced understanding of the complexities within the educational landscape. Just as a rose thrives despite constraints, Black women leaders possess the competencies to flourish within the educational milieu, and the resolve to dismantle the status quo for future generations.

Moreover, the experiences of Black women leaders align with the concept of "tempered radicals," as described by Alston and Meyerson. While those challenging colonialized systems and white supremacy cultures often face the choice of assimilation or departure, tempered radicalism offers an alternative path. Debra Meyerson's[3] research suggests that the tension between maintaining authenticity and navigating resistant organizations can serve as a catalyst for learning, leadership, and positive organizational transformation.

Based on 15 years of astute research and observation, the paradigm of "tempered radicals" illustrates that adaptive, inclusive, family-oriented, and ethically responsible workplaces are often cultivated not through revolutionary, but by building coalitions and collective understandings to strategically implement sustainable change. These individuals adeptly navigate the narrow path between conformity and rebellion, effectively introducing change through incremental steps. Unlike "untempered" radicals who often seek change through dramatic acts, tempered radicals advocate for transformative change through measured means. In this pursuit, they champion change not sporadically, but through daily dedication, fueled by conviction, patience, and unwavering courage. Black women leaders, embodying tempered radicalism, exemplify the harmonious convergence of authenticity and adaptation, signifying their role in fostering progressive transformation that disrupts the status quo and brings about sustainable educational reform.

Mirroring the vital role water plays in nourishing and supporting a rose's growth, gatekeepers such as boards, search consultants, and recruiters must actively nurture and empower Black women leaders. Gatekeepers possess the ability to establish a conducive environment for Black women leaders to prosper and achieve their maximum capabilities, much like water supplies the essential elements for a rose to thrive. This requires acknowledging and understanding the unique paths and experiences of these leaders, shaped by historical and ongoing systemic inequalities. Gatekeepers should act as allies, promoting access and growth.

Just as a rose thrives when pruned and nurtured, university preparatory programs must also play a crucial role in cultivating the success of Black women leaders. By designing cohorts and curricula that specifically address the unique needs and challenges faced by Black women leaders, these institutions can create a pipeline of empowered and transformative leaders. Such programs should be anchored in the rich tapestry of "herstory" and history, providing a deep understanding of the historical context that has shaped the experiences of Black women in leadership positions. This approach ensures leadership development is not only equitable but also culturally relevant and responsive.

Fundamentally, the "Roses from Concrete Leadership" model reflects the birth of a potent theoretical framework with significant implications for leadership intervention, development, and reform. It emerges from the interplay of dedication, insulation, and transformation, offering a roadmap for cultivating justice-oriented leadership.

The model's emphasis on unwavering dedication fortified by faith underscores the need for policies and interventions that address systemic barriers and nurture the spiritual and emotional well-being of Black women leaders. Recognizing and valuing the significance of these women's experiences, values, and inner strength offers a blueprint for allies to develop programs and policies that foster authenticity, resilience, conflict resolution skills, and the legitimacy of resistance, ultimately creating a more equitable and empowering leadership landscape.

Policymakers and educational institutions can leverage their power and allyship to design interventions that counteract the negative externalities of prejudice and bias. By embracing the power of collective support and shared experiences, we can create systems and practices that pave the way for a new era of educational leadership.

Finally, the transformative leadership—rooted in historical guidance, Black feminist thought, intersectionality, and tempered radicalism—demands a reimagining of traditional leadership development. By integrating these principles into leadership training programs, we can cultivate a new generation of leaders equipped to navigate complex challenges, and dismantle oppressive systems, paving the way for a collective and inclusive leadership approach.

Notes

1 Shakur, T. (1999). *The Rose that grew from concrete*. Pocket Books.
2 Swindler, A. (1986). Culture in action: Symbols and strategies. *American Sociological Review*, *51*(2), 273–286.
3 Meyerson, D. (2001). *Tempered radicals: How people use difference to inspire change at work*. Harvard Business School Press.

· 8 ·

SHAPING ORGANIZATIONAL AND EDUCATIONAL LEADERSHIP POLICY

The progress of the world will call for the best that all of us have to give.

—Mary McLeod Bethune[1]

This chapter underscores the dual nature of intersectionality, positioning it as both a comprehensive framework and an incisive analytical tool. It advocates for imperative social reforms and call on communities and individuals to embrace transformative organizational policy and growth. By methodically amplifying Black women leaders' voices and utilizing illuminating case studies, a nascent paradigm for social justice leadership has emerged, epitomized by the Roses from Concrete Leadership Model—an Afrocentric epistemological lens intricately woven with symbolism drawn from Tupac Shakur's evocative narrative.

Despite concerted efforts, the representation of Black women in superintendent and head roles remains stagnant. To address this, a multifaceted approach is required, beginning with robust data collection that empowers these leaders to share their experiences and advocate for change. Research is the key to progress, further study of this matter is greatly needed. Simultaneously, inclusive policies must be cultivated. These policies must not merely acknowledge the intricate interplay of racism and sexism but actively foster an environment that champions diverse perspectives and experiences, thereby nurturing an atmosphere conducive to understanding and transformation that goes beyond mere tolerance.

Addressing these systemic issues requires more than the efforts of those directly affected to fix it. Rather, it necessitates the active engagement of individuals who have benefited from these systems to become allies and advocates for educational reform, rather than remaining passive bystanders. Within this context, gatekeepers, including board members, recruiters, and individuals across racial and gender lines, play a pivotal role in effecting comprehensive transformations.

For boards, effective training involves understanding the challenges confronting Black women leaders. Ongoing research-based implicit bias trainings are crucial for decision-makers involved in hiring and promotions. These trainings help to uncover the nuances of unconscious biases, offering strategies to counteract their influence and ensure equitable decision-making. Additionally, fostering an environment that acknowledges their journey and contributions, while promoting growth and resilience, is imperative. This means taking proactive efforts to dismantle existing inequities and assuming accountability for instigating and meticulously executing organizational reforms.

Despite fluctuations in affirmative action policies, which have not historically benefited Black women to the same extent as white women, academic institutions must collaborate to create specialized programs meticulously tailored to address the unique challenges that Black women educational leaders face. Universities must be courageous in their recruitment endeavors, program design, and curriculum development, fostering an environment attuned to their journey and contributions. This understanding must translate into tangible support, including mentorship and resources specifically designed to facilitate a seamless transition into leadership roles, historically fraught with marginalization. Simultaneously, diversity by design principles must be firmly institutionalized, encouraging search committees to proactively seek diverse talent at each stage of recruitment. This includes outreach, hiring, compensation packages and onboarding practices, all with efforts to also support retention. Black women leaders must feel valued within the organization from the outset.

Crucially, comprehensive data collection and accountability are imperatives to combat organizational erasure. Systematically gathering and disseminating data concerning Black women in senior and executive roles propels the recognition of inequities and serves as the foundation for conscientious reforms.

Further Research Directions

The research and the Roses from Concrete leadership model presented in this book open promising areas for further exploration:

- **Expanding the Research Scope:** A larger-scale study involving a minimum of 30 participants across multiple states, to reinforce current findings and provide a broader understanding of the issue.
- **Grounded Theory Research:** A study utilizing grounded theory methodology to delve into Rose from Concrete leadership model, assessing its practical application in leadership development/intervention and mentoring programs for aspiring Black women leaders and potential impact on career trajectories.
- **Intersectionality as a Social Reform Tool:** An action research testing the effectiveness of intersectionality as a framework for driving social reform and managing organizational change within education leadership, focusing on the implementation of inclusive practices and leadership development programs.
- **Mixed-Methods Approach:** A study investigating factors influencing the retention and long-term success of Black women's in superintendency and headship positions, combining surveys and in-depth interviews.
- **Quantitative Study:** Surveying former students (of all races, ages 18 and older) who studied under Black women superintendents or heads of schools. This data would reveal how these experiences shaped students' learning journeys, perceptions of leadership, and future aspirations.

In addition to these, several comparative studies could offer valuable insights:

- **Compensation Disparities:** A comparison analysis of the salaries of black women superintendents and heads of schools with their male (Black and White men) and female (White women) counterparts, exploring potential gender and racial pay gaps.
- **Career Pathways:** A mixed-method study examining the career trajectories of women of color in educational leadership roles, exploring how intersectionality impacts their access to, experiences in, and retention within these positions.

Considering the global nature of education and how intersectionality also moves across national boundaries, it would also be valuable to:

- **International Perspectives:** Investigate how intersectionality influences the representation (or lack thereof) of Black women and women of color as heads of international schools in Africa, Asia, Europe, Australia, and the Americas, particularly in regions with large student populations of color. This research would examine the barriers and opportunities faced by these leaders in diverse global contexts.

The Urgency of Change

The lack of progress for Black women in the top executive leadership positions at both independent and public schools demands focused attention and open dialogue to drive change. It is a problem that this discourse remains limited and missing. States and national organizations cannot address a problem they do not know about or are not willing to learn about. To achieve systemic change, the focus must shift from "fixing" individuals to addressing the systemic biases that perpetuate the marginalization of Black women. Implicit bias and intercultural competency training can empower gatekeepers to understand the urgency and equip them with the tools to challenge existing inequalities. While the existing historical, political, and bureaucratic nature of school systems and their educational leaders do not inherently foster liberation, hope, empowerment, activism, risk, and social justice,[2] this very reality presents an opportunity to shift the paradigm.

Moving Towards Action

In the following chapter, we will delve into practical strategies and policy recommendations aimed at creating this desired equitable and inclusive educational ecosystem. This blueprint for change seeks to not only recognize but also celebrate and leverage the unique strengths and perspectives of marginalized groups in education, fostering an environment of hope and empowerment that can drive transformative change.

Notes

1 Bethune, M. M. (1935). What does American democracy mean to me? In D. A. Shannon (Ed.), *The negroes of America* (pp. 303–306). University of Chicago.
2 Shields, C. M. (2010). Transformative leadership: Working for equity in diverse contexts. *Educational Administration Quarterly*, 46(4), 558–589.

· 9 ·

BARRIERS TO BRIDGES: A BLUEPRINT FOR CHANGE

Success isn't about how much money you make. It's about the difference you make in people's lives.

—Michelle Obama[1]

In today's rapidly evolving educational landscape, fostering an inclusive leadership pipeline is no longer a "nice-to-have"—it's a strategic imperative. This is particularly crucial when considering the unique barriers faced by Black women in their pursuit of school executive leadership positions, as highlighted in the research presented throughout this book. Michelle Obama's words resonate deeply with this imperative. True success blossoms not from personal gain, but from the seeds of positive change we sow in the lives of others. Much like roses that defiantly bloom from concrete, transformative leadership emerges from recognizing and nurturing the potential within each individual, regardless of their background.

In the spirit of cultivating transformative leadership, this chapter guides you through strategies for dismantling the barriers that specifically stifle the advancement of Black women, while recognizing that these strategies can serve as a blueprint and also be applied to support other underrepresented groups. Having explored the systemic obstacles that hinder equitable opportunity, we now turn our focus towards actionable solutions to foster a vibrant and equitable environment for all.

An inclusive leadership pipeline is not merely a box to be ticked; it is the lifeblood that nourishes an organization's capacity for innovation, resilience, and sustainable growth. Consider this chapter your compass, guiding you through the strategies that attract, develop, and empower Black women leaders. We'll explore the importance of inclusive recruitment practices, mentorship and sponsorship programs, leadership development initiatives, and creating a culture of belonging. By implementing these strategies, you can unlock the full potential of your workforce and drive sustainable success for your organization. Together, we'll transform the ideals of equity and inclusion into a vibrant reality, building a brighter future for your schools and the communities they serve.

Strategies for the Gatekeepers

Efforts to promote inclusivity and dismantle obstacles for Black women educational, leadership necessitate collaborative efforts among school board recruiters, and search consultants. These critical gatekeepers play a pivotal role in the initial phases of change, in having Black women gain access to superintendent and head of school roles.

Boards, recruiters, and search consultants must collaborate to create and enforce policies that openly advocate for diversity and inclusion in the recruitment and hiring of heads and superintendents. Gatekeepers can also serve as sponsors, allowing them to diversify outreach and intentionally seek out diverse talent that can enhance and advance the community's needs. To do this, implicit bias and diversity training are necessary for these gatekeepers. They will need to re-evaluate their understanding of the "ideal candidate" and "best fit," challenging established notions about the "perfect" candidate and embracing a more holistic view of qualifications. This includes recognizing the value of lived experience, cultural competence, and a demonstrated commitment to equity and inclusion. Additionally, recruiters and search consultants must be vulnerable, acknowledging biases in standard hiring practices and prioritizing the pursuit of excellence over rigid ideas of the "right fit." Recognizing diverse pathways to success is crucial.

Succession planning and talent management are critical in ensuring organizational success. Hiring, sustaining, and supporting the superintendent or head of school is the most important responsibility of a school board—as this crucial responsibility sustains the school's livelihood, mission, vision, and viability[2]. School boards hold a unique responsibility as their primary role is to hire, evaluate, and retain superintendents and heads of school. This positions them as essential agents in fostering inclusive leadership. Recognizing that the head of school/superintendent is their sole employee, the board's duty is to wholeheartedly support her, as she is the visible face and leader of board-approved changes that seek to move the school forward. Boards must actively participate in onboarding new Black women superintendents and heads, ensuring a smooth transition into their roles. This includes providing access to coaches and mentors who can offer guidance, support, and strategies for navigating systemic barriers. Such mentorship is not only crucial for accessing leadership roles but also for thriving within them. Prioritizing onboarding, transitioning, and retention processes is essential for effective workforce development. Creating a nurturing and inclusive environment for new superintendents and heads is crucial for fostering an inclusive culture that, in turn, enhances their retention.

Furthermore, boards must invest in ongoing leadership development opportunities for themselves and the broader school community. This commitment to continuous learning ensures that all stakeholders are equipped with the knowledge and skills to build an inclusive and equitable educational environment. Engaging the community in this process is vital, as it fosters a sense of shared ownership and empowers diverse voices to contribute to the school's vision and goals.

Cultivating an environment that promotes innovation is vital for optimizing talent and achieving institutional success. This involves recognizing and celebrating the individual differences and unique abilities of all community members, creating a space where originality and exceptional quality can flourish. Utilizing data from climate surveys and evaluations can provide valuable insights into the experiences of Black women leaders, enabling institutions to identify areas for improvement and implement targeted interventions to support their success.

Strategies for University and Education Leadership Programs

In the pursuit of transformative education leadership, universities and educational leadership programs wield immense influence in shaping the next generation of leaders. Their role is pivotal in determining the diversity and inclusivity of leadership positions such as superintendency and headship.

First and foremost, these programs must be intentionally designed with diversity in mind. This involves the deliberate creation of diverse graduate and doctorate cohorts, embracing the concept of "diversity by design." This approach seeks to foster a rich tapestry of talents and perspectives, incorporating individuals from diverse backgrounds, races, genders, and experiences. Beyond building a robust pipeline, it cultivates a culture of reciprocal learning that is culturally responsive and promotes allyship.

Furthermore, universities need to champion scholarship initiatives that address access and inequities. This entails actively seeking out and empowering Black women and other marginalized professionals with strong leadership potential and intercultural competencies. By thinking outside the box and securing funding for fellowships and scholarships, universities can create a supportive environment for aspiring leaders from underrepresented groups.

The heart of this educational revolution lies in its dedication to creating cultural responsiveness. This commitment manifests in the creation of courses and curricula that foster intercultural competencies and equip leaders with the tools to navigate diverse educational landscapes. The Black Feminist Leadership Model (BFLM), as discussed in Chapter 7, functions as an exemplary framework that fosters the development of trailblazers, supporters, and efficient leadership teams. It fosters a culture of high expectations for inclusion and holds both leaders and communities accountable for success. When incorporated in university and leadership development curricula, the BFLM becomes a beacon guiding us toward inclusive and effective leadership practices, transcending boundaries, and honoring diversity in thought and experience.

Additionally, educational leadership programs must integrate more curriculum elements that unravel the complexities of board governance. Infusing more courses and practical exposure to governance, finance, and the operational components of the superintendency-headship role, offers a holistic approach that prepares emerging leaders with a versatile set of abilities. This empowerment allows individuals to effectively navigate the complex landscape of educational institutions, creating environments that promote fairness, inclusiveness, and efficient management.

Moreover, these programs should prioritize fiduciary, strategic, and generative functions, emphasizing the importance of a collaborative superintendent-board partnership. This partnership is often likened to a dance—a graceful, adaptive collaboration that harmonizes with the rhythm and tempo to creatively bring about change at the right speed. This metaphor symbolizes the necessary qualities of adaptability and mutual benefit that are essential for achieving success in today's educational ecosystem.

Lastly, university administrators hold a crucial position as catalysts and architects of progress. Collaborating with diversity and inclusion specialists is essential in guiding curriculum design and providing training to advance the learning of existing faculty. The ultimate goal goes beyond representation; it calls for the cultivation of leaders who authentically reflect on and ardently advocate for the diverse student populations they serve. In this transformative journey, diversity and inclusion specialists are key partners, contributing to a culture of continuous growth and development.

Strategies for Researchers and Practitioners

Researchers play a pivotal in advancing theory and practice in organizational, human resource, leadership, and policy development. Engaging in theory-building case studies that explore the intersectionality of race, gender, and power dynamics within educational leadership is recommended. Collaborating with practitioners ensures practical relevance in addressing challenges faced by Black women superintendents and heads of schools. Encouraging interdisciplinary research enriches the understanding of these challenges, providing a comprehensive perspective.

In qualitative theory-building case-study research, a comprehensive inquiry into existing theory, contextual understanding, and real-world practices is crucial. The findings from such studies can enhance, restructure, and introduce new theoretical understandings, which are particularly essential in addressing recurring challenges in the field of human resources development.[3] In fact, researchers advocate for theory-generating and theory-testing methodologies in case-study research, establishing connections between theory and research in real-world practice.[4] To address the underrepresentation of Black women in school leadership positions, the application of theory-building case studies is therefore recommended.

This book aims to overcome limitations in qualitative theory-building case-study research by providing implications for both theory-testing and theory-building rooted in inclusive and diverse epistemologies. Theory, research, and practice involve an interactive connection, requiring researchers to exercise awareness, discerning judgment, varied epistemologies, and sensitivity to specific contexts and marginalized experiences.

Researchers, practitioners, and educational leaders each offer unique contributions to understanding real-world phenomena, and hold the power to implement strategies that can advance sustainable change. In the pursuit of justice, school leaders, governing boards, university administrators, recruiters, and sitting superintendents-heads must be active agents, not mere spectators. Mere moral inclination is insufficient; justice requires concrete action. Implementing justice within schools involves safeguarding, healing, and restoration. All stakeholders, particularly educational and governance leaders, bear the responsibility of translating these principles into action, ensuring equity and justice realization.

Strategies for Human Resource Development (HRD)

Human resources professionals play a crucial role in enacting justice within educational institutions by actively collecting and scrutinizing data to identify disparities or inequalities in recruitment, advancement, and disciplinary measures. Armed with this information, HR managers can devise staffing plans that help school leaders and boards proactively identify and recruit talent that specifically aligns with the direction and needs of the school and its community. Furthermore, HRD policies and practices should directly address exclusionary and discriminatory behaviors, rectify biases, and ensure equitable treatment for all individuals.

Strategies for Human Resource Development (HRD) are vital for building a robust and inclusive leadership pipeline. Critically, superintendents and heads of school must have recourse against discriminatory treatment, ensuring a safe and supportive environment for all aspiring leaders. This includes implementing clear policies against discrimination and harassment, establishing confidential reporting mechanisms, and providing resources for those who have experienced unfair treatment. Additionally, HRD initiatives should focus on cultivating a culture of diversity and inclusion through targeted recruitment efforts, mentorship programs, leadership development opportunities, and ongoing training on unconscious bias and cultural competency. By fostering an inclusive environment where all individuals feel valued and empowered to succeed, schools can attract and retain a diverse pool of talented leaders who are equipped to meet the challenges of the 21st century.

Establishing clear reporting procedures and the implementation of restorative practices are indispensable for fostering fairness and equity within schools. All members of the school community, including students, staff, and administrators, must have a formal system to report instances of prejudice, discrimination, harassment, and mistreatment. Effective child protection protocols and harassment prevention processes, already proven successful in many schools and institutions, can serve as models for preventing and addressing microaggressions, gaslighting, and other discriminatory behaviors. This necessitates state departments of education, accrediting agencies, and governing bodies establishing clear protocols to support Black women leaders in reporting and addressing these issues. These protocols should ensure confidentiality, impartiality, and timely resolution of complaints.

Advocating for restorative practices within the institution contributes to cultivating a safe school climate. Restorative methods prioritize the restoration of harm caused by incidents, fostering accountability and encouraging open dialogues for comprehension and healing, moving beyond punitive measures. Additionally, inclusion specialists can play a vital role in working collaboratively with all these institutions to tailor solutions that address the specific needs and challenges faced by Black women leaders. Their expertise can help guide the development and implementation of comprehensive anti-discrimination policies, training programs, and restorative practices, emphasizing the urgency and necessity of substantial transformation within the educational system.

Justice is Love in Action

Essentially, the collective actions and inactions of the school community ultimately determine the prioritization of justice and equity in decision-making processes. The superintendent-head of the school and human resources directors must collaborate to establish rules and procedures that not only foster fairness but also hold individuals accountable for harmful conduct. This collaboration is essential to creating a safe space that nurtures and cultivates Black women and other marginalized talent in our schools, building a pipeline for future diverse school leaders, including superintendents and heads of school. And essentially, the board of trustees hold the power to ensure that the school's mission aligns with the concepts of justice and equity, actively supporting and seeking funding for activities that advance these ideals.

To foster justice in schools, boards and school leaders can work to enhance the multicultural competence of community members, implement restorative practices, and strengthen their capacity to address social justice concerns within the school community. Collectively, the school community has the capacity to build a culture centered around equity, fairness and love, actively demonstrating compassion, liberation, healing, and growth. This collective effort empowers all stakeholders and ensures that justice is not merely an abstract concept but a lived reality within the school environment.

Notes

1 Michelle Obama Convention Speech, September 4, 2012.
2 Donna Orem, "Making Room for Strategy," *The NAIS Head Search Handbook: A Strategy Guide for the Search Committee* (2018).
3 Lynham, S. A. (2000). Theory building in the human resource development profession. *Human Resource Development Quarterly*, *11*(2), 159–178.
4 Rule, P., & John, V. M. (2015). A necessary dialogue. *International Journal of Qualitative Methods*, *14*(4), 160940691561157. https://doi.org/10.1177/1609406915611575.

· 10 ·

CONCLUDING REFLECTIONS: NURTURING A DIVERSE LEADERSHIP PIPELINE

Not everything that is faced can be changed, but nothing can be changed until it is faced.

—James Baldwin[1]

This book has illuminated the multifaceted nature of intersectionality, positioning it as both a comprehensive framework and a potent analytical tool. It extends beyond advocating for essential social reforms, urging communities and individuals to embrace growth and transformation within the educational sphere. By amplifying the voices of Black women leaders and showcasing compelling case studies, a blueprint for social justice leadership emerges—the Roses from Concrete or Black Feminist Leadership Model. This innovative approach, rooted in Afrocentric epistemology and interwoven with the symbolism of Tupac Shakur's poem, underscores the urgency to address deeply rooted disparities.

The persistent underrepresentation of Black women in the superintendent and head of school positions necessitates decisive actions. Research stands as a cornerstone of progress, and the path forward requires broader exploration. While this book provides foundational insights, future studies should expand the discourse. Despite the modest sample size of six, reflecting a fraction of the Black female superintendents-heads in New York public and independent schools, forthcoming research should amplify more voices, including those of other marginalized groups with intersecting identities.

Initiating this journey involves meticulous data collection, empowering Black women leaders to share their truths, and harnessing their transformative capacities. This, in turn, enriches the educational landscape for the holistic benefit of students and society as a whole.

Addressing intersectionality empowers individuals to deconstruct prevailing inequities. This process involves grasping the Roses from Concrete model, which empowers individuals and encourages them to dismantle operational structures that perpetuate biases. Engaging White allies in this endeavor is pivotal, as their support forges a pathway for progress. Central to this is shedding the masks that obstruct the acceptance of race, gender, and social politics. By taking concrete measures to dismantle biases, the leadership pipeline within schools can evolve into a more inclusive space for Black women and other marginalized groups.

In tackling the marginalization of Black women, systemic change emerges as an imperative. Implicit bias, intercultural competency, and culturally responsive training are vital tools for gatekeepers and boards to transition from passive observers to active allies in effecting positive transformation. While history, politics, and bureaucracy might fall short in inspiring liberation and justice, the experiences of Black women herald a transformative paradigm shift in leadership.

These women's journeys and insights instill a courageous spirit, challenging allies to harness this courage in building partnerships for organizational change. Allies are called upon to cultivate self-awareness and bravery, recognizing the dynamic nature of culture. Schools as organizations, must incorporate an understanding of how colonization, oppression, and racism impact cultural groups and individuals. This recognition necessitates a shift toward collaboration, partnership, interactive learning, and perpetual growth. Integral to this shift is acknowledging the imperative to address power dynamics and racism, as failure to do so can perpetuate more harm to marginalized groups.[2]

Against the backdrop of a history marked by white supremacy and colonization, many spaces remain inherently unsafe for Black women leaders to truly flourish and authentically express themselves. To rebalance power dynamics and foster safety, allies must acknowledge their role, take responsibility, and leverage their power and privilege to actively dismantle systems of oppression and create communities where everyone feels valued, respected, and empowered to thrive, regardless of their cultural and socially intersecting background. They cultivate the knowledge, attitudes, and skills needed for equitable collaborations across a multitude of cultures. "Creating safe environments transcends physical security; it involves fostering respect, shared understanding, knowledge exchange, and collective growth with dignity."[3]

The concept of intersectionality recognizes that human lives cannot be fully understood by examining single categories such as gender, race, sexuality, or socioeconomic status. Instead, lives are complex and shaped by a multitude of interconnected factors and social dynamics. Understanding this, allies must shoulder responsibility and foster partnerships that nurture safe spaces where diverse identities are honored and celebrated, fostering collaborations that promote equity and inclusion.

The journey towards an equitable leadership landscape continues, fueled by resilience, activism, and the shared vision. By embracing the principles and strategies outlined in this book, we can collectively dismantle the barriers that have long held back Black women and other marginalized groups, paving the way for a more just and equitable future in educational leadership. But it is not enough to simply create opportunities; we must also ensure that Black women are visibly represented in these leadership spaces. This representation matters not only for the young learners who see themselves reflected in their leaders, but also for the broader community, as it fosters greater understanding, adaptability, and cultural competence. By celebrating and empowering Black women in educational leadership, we create a ripple effect that inspires future generations and contributes to a more inclusive and equitable world for all.

Notes

1 Baldwin, J. (1962, January 14). As much truth as one can bear; to speak out about the world as it is, says James Baldwin, is the writer's job as much of the truth as one can bear. *The New York Times*, p. BR11.
2 Sakamoto, I. (2007). An anti-oppressive approach to cultural competence. *Canadian Social Work Review / Revue Canadienne de Service Social*, *24*(1), 105–114. http://www.jstor.org/stable/41669865.
3 Williams, R. (1999). Cultural safety—what does it mean for our work practice? *Australian and New Zealand Journal of Public Health*, *23*(2), 213–214. https://doi.org/10.1111/j.1467-842X.1999.tb01240, p. 213.

FURTHER READING

Abrams, K. M., & Gaiser, T. J. (2016). Online focus groups. In N. G. Fielding, R. M. Lee, & G. Blank (Eds.), *The Sage handbook of online research methods* (2nd ed., pp. 435–450). Sage.

Alston, J. A. (1999). Climbing hills and mountains: Black women making it to the superintendency. In C. C. Brunner (Ed.), *Sacred dreams: Women and the superintendency* (pp. 79–90). State University of New York.

Alston, J. A. (2000). Missing from action: Where are the Black female school superintendents? *Urban Education*, *35*(5), 525–531.

Alston, J. A. (2005). Tempered radicals and servant leaders: Black females persevering in the superintendency. *Educational Administration Quarterly*, *41*(4), 675–688.

Baldwin, J. (1962, January 14). As much truth as one can bear; to speak out about the world as it is, says James Baldwin, is the writer's job as much of the truth as one can bear. *The New York Times*, p. BR11.

Björk, L. (2000). Introduction: Women in the superintendency—advances in research and theory. *Educational Administration Quarterly*, *36*(1), 5–17.

Blount, J. M. (1998). *Destined to rule the schools: Women and the superintendency 1873–1995*. State University of New York.

Bowen, G. A. (2009). Document analysis as a qualitative research method. *Qualitative Research Journal*, *9*(2), 27–40.

Brown, A. R. (2014). The recruitment and retention of African American women as public school superintendents. *Journal of Black Studies*, *45*(6), 573–593. https://doi.org/10.1177/0021934714542157

Brunner, C. C. (2008). Invisible, limited, and emerging discourse: Research practices that restrict and/or increase access for women and persons of color to the superintendency. *Journal of School Leadership, 13*(4), 428–450. https://doi.org/10.1177/105268460301300405

Brunner, C. C., & Peyton-Caire, L. (2000). Seeking representation supporting Black female graduate students who aspire to the superintendency. *Urban Education, 35*(5), 532–548.

Burton, L. J., Cyr, D., & Weiner, J. M. (2020). "Unbroken, but bent": Gendered racism in school leadership. *Frontiers in Education, 5*. https://doi.org/10.3389/feduc.2020.00052

Carbado, D. W., Crenshaw, K. W., Mays, V. M., & Tomlinson, B. (2013). Intersectionality: Mapping the movements of a theory. *Du Bois Review, 10*(2), 303–312. https://doi.org/10.1017/S1742058X13000349

Collins, P. H. (1989). The social construction of Black feminist thought. *Signs, 14*(4), 745–773. http://www.jstor.org/stable/3174683

Costello, A. (2021). *Long Island 2021 school superintendent salaries ranked.* Garden City Patch. https://patch.com/new-york/gardencity/long-island-2021-school-superintendent-salaries-ranked

Crenshaw, K. (1989). Demarginalizing the intersection of race and sex: A Black feminist critique of antidiscrimination doctrine, feminist theory and antiracist politics. *University of Chicago Legal Forum, 1989*(1).

Crenshaw, K. (1991). Mapping the margins: Intersectionality, identity politics, and violence against women of color. *Stanford Law Review, 43*(6), 1241–1299. https://doi.org/10.2307/1229039

Creswell, J. W., & Poth, C. N. (2018). *Qualitative inquiry and research design* (4th ed.). Sage.

Department of Health and Human Services & The National Commission for Protection of Human Subjects of Biomedical and Behavioral Research. (1978). *The Belmont report. Ethical principles and guidelines for the protection of human subjects of research.*

Dooley, L. M. (2002). Case study research and theory building. *Advances in Developing Human Resources, 4*(3), 335–354.

Duckworth, A. (2016). *Grit: The power of passion and perseverance.* Scribner/Simon & Schuster.

Eisenhardt, K. M. (1989). Building theory from case study research. *Academy of Management Review, 14*(4), 532–550.

Eisenhardt, K. M., & Graebner, M. E. (2007). Theory building from cases: Opportunities and challenges. *Academy of Management Journal, 50*(1), 25–32.

Fitzgerald, T. (2006). Walking between two worlds. *Educational Management Administration & Leadership, 34*(2), 201–213.

Glass, T. E. (1992). *The 1992 study of the American superintendency: American's education leaders in a time of reform.* American Association of School Administrators.

Glass, T. E. (2000). Where are all the women superintendents? *School Administrator, 57*, 28–32.

Glass, T. E., Bjork, L. G., & Brunner, C. C. (2000). *The study of the American school superintendency 2000: A look at the superintendent of education in the new millennium.* American Association of School Administrators.

Glass, T. E., & Franceschini, L. A. (2007). *The state of the American school superintendency: A mid-decade study.* American Association of School Administrators.

Godfrey, E. B., & Burson, E. (2018). Interrogating the intersections: How intersectional perspectives can inform developmental scholarship on critical consciousness. *New Directions for Child and Adolescent Development, 161*, 17–38.

Gordon, E. W., Miller, F., & Rollock, D. (1990). Coping with communicentric bias in knowledge production in the social sciences. *Educational Researcher, 19*(3), 14–19.

Hurston, Z. N. (1942). *Dust tracks on a road*. Arno.

Jackson, B. L. (1999). Getting inside history—against all odds: African-American women school superintendents. In C. C. Brunner (Ed.), *Sacred dreams: Women in the superintendency* (pp. 141–160). State University of New York.

Jackson, J., & Shakeshaft, C. (2003, April 22). *The pool of African-American candidates for the superintendency* [Paper presentation]. American Education Research Association Annual Meeting, Chicago, IL, United States. https://files.eric.ed.gov/fulltext/ED479479.pdf

Jean-Marie, G., Williams, V. A., & Sherman, S. L. (2009). Black women's leadership experiences: Examining the intersectionality of race and gender. *Advances in Developing Human Resources, 11*(5), 562–581. https://doi.org/10.1177/1523422309351836

Johnson, K. G. (2013). *African American women superintendents: Pathways to success* [Doctoral dissertation, Louisiana State University]. https://digitalcommons.lsu.edu/gradschool_dissertations/2069/

Kawulich, B. B. (2005). Participant observation as data collection method. *Forum: Qualitative Social Research*, 6(2), Art. 43. https://www.qualitative-research.net/index.php/fqs/article/view/466/996

Kennedy. A. M. (2019). *African American women superintendents: Are we being marginalized?* [Doctoral dissertation, Morgan State University]. https://mdsoar.org/bitstream/handle/11603/17892/Kennedy_AM_2019.pdf?sequence=1

Kowalski, T. J., McCord, R. S., Pretson, G. J., Young, P. I., & Ellerson, N. M. (2011). *The American school superintendent: 2010 decennial study*. Rowman & Littlefield/American Association of School Superintendents (AASA).

Lune, H., & Berg, B. L. (2017). *Qualitative research methods for the social sciences* (9th ed.). Pearson.

Lynham, S. A. (2000). Theory building in the Human Resource Development Profession. *Human Resource Development Quarterly, 11*(2), 159–178.

Maxwell, J. A. (2013). *Qualitative research design: An interactive approach* (3rd ed.). Sage.

McCulloch, G. (2004). The joy of life: Doing documentary research. In *Documentary research: In education, history, and the social sciences* (pp. 25–43). Routledge Falmer.

Mcintosh, P. (2003). White privilege: Unpacking the invisible knapsack. https://www.wcwonline.org/Publications-by-title/white-privilege-unpacking-the-invisible-knapsack-2

Méndez-Morse, S. (1999). Redefinition of self: Mexican-American women becoming superintendents. In C. Cryss Brunner (Ed.), *Sacred dreams: Women and the superintendency* (pp. 125–140). State University of New York.

Meyerson, D. (2001). *Tempered radicals: How people use difference to inspire change at work*. Harvard Business School Press.

Miles, M. B., Huberman, M. A., & Saldaña, J. (2020). *Qualitative data analysis: A methods sourcebook* (4th ed.). Sage.

Moffitt, U., Juang, L. P., & Syed, M. (2020). Intersectionality and youth identity development research in Europe. *Frontiers in Psychology*, *11*, 78. https://doi.org/10.3389/fpsyg.2020.00078

Merriam, S. B., & Tisdell, E. J. (2016). Chapter 6: Being a careful observer. In *Qualitative research: A guide to design and implementation* (pp. 137–161). Jossey-Bass.

Natow, R. S. (2019). Online qualitative data sources for federal regulatory policy studies. *American Behavioral Scientist*, 63(3), 315–332.

Natow, R. S. (2020). The use of triangulation in qualitative studies employing elite interviews. *Qualitative Research*, 20(2), 160–173. https://doi.org/10.1177/1468794119830077

National Public Radio (NPR). (2012, September 5). *Transcript: Michelle Obama's convention speech*. NPR. https://www.npr.org/2012/09/04/160578836/transcript-michelle-obamas-convention-speech

Orem, D. (2018). Making Room for Strategy. In *The NAIS Head Search Handbook: A Strategy Guide for the Search Committee*. National Association of Independent Schools.

Ortiz, F. I. (2000). Who controls succession in the superintendency? A minority perspective. *Urban Education*, 35(5), 557–566.

Ortiz, F. I. (2001). Using social capital in interpreting the careers of three Latina superintendents. *Educational Administration Quarterly*, 37(1), 58–85.

Pallas, A. M. (2001). Preparing education doctoral students for epistemological diversity. *Educational Researcher*, 30(5), 6–11.

Patton, M. Q. (2002). *Qualitative research & evaluation methods*. Sage.

Revere, A. B. (1986, April). *A description of Black female school superintendents*. *The Black superintendency: Challenge or crisis?* Symposium conducted at the meeting of the American Educational Research Association of San Francisco, CA.

Revere, A. B. (1987). Black women superintendents in the United States: 1984–1985. *Journal of Negro Education*, 56(4), 510–520.

Richards, N. N. (2023). *A theory-building case study examining the relevance and impact of intersectionality on the lived experiences of Black women superintendents and heads of school* [Doctoral dissertation, Hofstra University]. ProQuest Dissertations Publishing. https://www.proquest.com/docview/30310396

Rodriguez, S. A. (2014). *Extraordinary women in Texas: A phenomenological study of Mexican American female superintendents* [Doctoral dissertation, Texas State University].

Rubin, H. J., & Rubin, I. S. (2012). Chapter 8: Structure of the response interview. In *Qualitative interviewing: The art of hearing data* (pp. 115–129). Sage.

Rule, P., & John, V. M. (2015). A necessary dialogue. *International Journal of Qualitative Methods*, *14*(4), 160940691561157. https://doi.org/10.1177/1609406915611575

Sakamoto, I. (2007). An Anti-oppressive approach to cultural competence. *Canadian Social Work Review / Revue Canadienne de Service Social*, 24(1), 105–114. http://www.jstor.org/stable/41669865

Shakeshaft, C. (1989). *Women in education administration*. Sage.

Shakur, T. (1999). *The Rose that grew from concrete*. New York: Pocket Books.

Shields, C. M. (2010). Transformative leadership: Working for equity in diverse contexts. *Educational Administration Quarterly*, 46(4), 558–589.

Shields, S. A. (2008). Gender: An intersectionality perspective. *Sex Roles*, *59*, 301–311. https://doi.org/10.1007/s11199-008-9501-8

Suggs Mason, B. (2021). *Intersectionality and the leadership of Black women superintendents* [Doctoral dissertation, University of Illinois Urbana–Champaign].

Sullivan, E. (2019). *#SuperintentendentsSoWhite: Three takeaways from the annual survey of school leaders*. EdSurge. https://www.edsurge.com/news/2019-02-19-superintendentssowhite-three-takeaways-fro m-the-annual-survey-of-school-leaders

Suri, H. (2011). Purposeful sampling in qualitative research synthesis. *Qualitative Research Journal*, *11*, 63–75.

Swindler, A. (1986). Culture in action: Symbols and strategies. *American Sociological Review*, *51*(2), 273–286.

Taylor, T. S. (2007). Battling bias: It's still about race. But it's not in your face. *Essence*, *4*, 164–167.

Tillman, B. A., & Cochran, L. L. (2000). Desegregating urban school administration: A pursuit of equity for Black women superintendents. *Education and Urban Society*, *33*(1), 44–59.

Wiley, K., Bustamante, R., Ballenger, J., & Poknick, B. (2017). African American women superintendents in Texas: An exploration of challenges and supports. *Journal of School Administration Research and Development*, *2*(1), 18–24.

Williams, R. (1999). Cultural safety—what does it mean for our work practice? *Australian and New Zealand Journal of Public Health*, *23*(2), 213–214. https://doi.org/10.1111/j.1467-842X.1999.tb01240.x

Made in the USA
Middletown, DE
07 September 2024

60577559R00076